French Grammar for Beginners

The Most Complete Textbook and Workbook for French Learners

By Frederic Bibard

No part of this book including the audio material may be copied, reproduced, transmitted or distributed in any form without the prior written permission of the author. For permission requests, write to: contact@talkinfrench.com

Also available:

French Short Stories for Beginners

TABLE OF CONTENTS

A FOREWORD

French is the second most widely taught foreign language in the world. Weirdly, however, and despite the staggering amount of material available on the topic, there is a distinct lack of resources that approach the subject in a fun and lively manner.

This is the glaring omission I attempt to cover in my website, the subsequent emails, newsletters, and of course, this book. Since the conception of my website www. talkinfrench.com, my team and I have endeavoured to approach learning French in an unconventional way by making it engaging, friendly, and injected with a little bit of humour here and there.

What others call "tried-and-tested", I call "old and boring", and I am trying my best to do away with it even if it kills me (figuratively speaking, of course).

Let's face it, learning a new language is hard. I'm not going to sugarcoat my words and say that you'll breeze through it all like the genius that you are. Well, I could be wrong and you could be a genuine linguistic genius of some sort. But definitely not everyone is.

To achieve a certain level of fluency in a language, the average person has to study it for at least 800 hours. This length of time can seem unbearable to a lot of people and the tendency to quit when the going gets tough and boring is high. To prevent this, I want you to build a habit for learning French. Together, we can work hand in hand to achieve this. Moreover, once you have created the learning habit, I assure you, it only gets easier.

This book is structured in such a way that habit creation and fun are carefully combined and lovingly married together to create a gorgeous offspring known as language learning. (Are you excited yet? I sure am.)

I hope you'll join us for this amazing ride. So come on, get on board with me for thirty days and let's make learning French a habit.

À bientôt !

Frederic, Founder of Talkinfrench.com

Important note: If you want the audio, go to page 225 .

DAY 1
GREETINGS

...or how a quick smile is never enough.

Greetings are one of the very first things you should consider when learning a new language. Whether a trip to a French-speaking destination is on the horizon for you or not, you should always be armed and ready with these indispensable words.

In some countries, smiling or nodding your head in acknowledgment can already be considered a form of greeting. This is not the case in French. The polite way to go about your day is to utter a quick hello to everyone you come across, including everyone within earshot in public places. Each conversation is also expected to begin with a proper greeting.

Ready yet? Here are the greetings that should be second nature to you, like they are to the native French.

Track 1

Bonjour !	[bohn-zoor]	*Hello!* *Good morning!* *Good day!*
Bonsoir !	[bohn-swar]	*Good Evening!*
Salut !	[sa-lew]	*Hello/Hi! (informal)*

Aside from the usual "*hellos*", it is also quite common to ask "*how's it going?*" or "*how are you?*"

Comment ça va ?	[koh-mmahn-sah-vah]	*How are things?* *How's it going?*
Comment vas-tu ?	[koh-mmahn-vah-too]	*How are you? (informal)*
Comment allez-vous ?	[kohn-mmahn-t-ahlaayvoo]	*How are you? (formal)*

Ça va ?	[sah-vah]	*How's it going? (informal)*

And this is how you reply.

Bien, merci.	[bee-anh mair-see]	*Well, thank you.*
Très bien.	[tray bee-anh]	*Very well.*
Tout va bien.	[too vah bee-anh]	*Everything is going well.*
Pas très bien.	[pah tray bee-anh]	*Not very well.*
Pas trop mal.	[pah trow mahl]	*Not too bad.*

After replying, you should also ask how the other person is doing. You can do this by simply saying:

Et toi ?	[eh toa]	*And you? (informal)*
Et vous ?	[eh voo]	*And you? (formal)*

formal

When you've exhausted all the "*hellos*" and it's time to move on, here's what you can say.

Au revoir !	[oh ruh-vwar]	*Goodbye!*
Salut !	[sah-loo]	*Bye! (informal)*
À bientôt !	[ah bianh-toh]	*See you soon!*
Bonne journée !	[bonn zhoor-nayh]	*Good day! Have a nice day!*
Bonne nuit !	[bohn-nwee]	*Good night! (used only when you're about to go to sleep)*

And finally...

Kissing the cheeks is also expected, but only if you are already familiar with the person. If you're meeting him or her for the very first time, you're better off simply shaking hands. Now, the number of kisses can be quite confusing. In Paris, it's generally four, but in the rest of France, it's two. In other French-speaking countries, it also varies. The best thing to do is just observe before you dive in.

LET'S PRACTICE!

Exercise 1.1 - Fill in the blanks in this dialogue:

Formal discussion (your boss):

Vous (*you*): _Bonjour_ Monsieur!

Votre chef (*your boss*): Bonjour, _comment allez_? vous

Vous (*you*): _Tres bien,_ Et vous?

Votre chef (*your boss*): _Tres bien_, merci.

Informal discussion (friends):

Vous (*you*): _Salut_ !

Votre ami (*your friend*): Salut XXX, _comment ca_ ? va

Vous (*you*): Oui, ça va. _Et toi_ ?

Votre ami (*your friend*): _Bien_, bonne journée.

> **Fun fact:** French is the second most widely taught foreign language in the world after English.

Exercise 1.2 - Choose the correct answer:

1. Rachel is a friend of Marie. She would ask her:

   (a.) Comment vas-tu ?   b. Comment allez-vous ?

2. It's morning. Paul wants to say good morning to Mark. He would say:

   a. Bonsoir !   b. Bonne journée.   (c.) Bonjour !

3. To wish someone good night, you would say:

   a. Bonsoir !   (b.) Bonne nuit.   c. Bonne journée !

4. To say goodbye, you should say:

   a. Salut !   b. Ça va ?   (c.) Au revoir.

5. You want to ask your boss how he is. You say:

   a. Comment vas-tu ?   (b.) Comment allez-vous ?

Exercise 1.3 - Translate from French to English and vice versa:

French	English
1. Bonjour !	*Good day!*
2. ...... *comment ca va?*	How are things?
3. ...... *Bien, merci*	Well, thank you.
4. Pas très bien.	*Not very good.*
5. ...... *Et toi ?*	And you? (informal)
6. Au revoir.	*Goodbye.*

Exercise 1.4 - This is a conversation between you and a friend (informal). Make the necessary changes so that it becomes a conversation between you and your boss (formal):

Vous (*you*): Salut ! Comment vas-tu ?   - *Bonjour! comment allez-vous?*

Votre ami (*your friend*): Bien. Et toi ? - *Bien. Et vous?*

Vous (*you*): Pas mal. À bientôt !   - *Pas mal. Au revoir.*

Votre ami (*your friend*): Salut !   - *Bonne journée*

Exercise 1.5 - Translate from French to English and vice versa:

French	English
1. ...... *Bon soirée*	Good evening.
2. ...... *Comment ca va*	How are you? (informal)
3. Très bien.	...... *very good*
4. ...... *Pas mal*	Not too bad.
5. ...... *Et toi?*	And you? (formal)
6. À bientôt !	...... *See you later!*

Exercise 1.6 - Translate this conversation from English to French:

English	French
You: Good morning. How's it going?	**Vous:** Bonjour. comment ça va?
Your friend: Not too bad. And you?	**Votre ami:** Pas mal. Et va toi?
You: Everything is going well. See you soon!	**Vous:** Tout et bien. A bientôt!
Your friend: Bye!	**Votre ami:** Salut

Exercise 1.7 - Choose the correct answer:

1. Your friend asked you, "*Ça va ?*" You're not feeling very well. You would say:

    a. Très bien.   b. Pas trop mal.   (c.) Pas très bien.

2. To wish someone a good day, you would say:

    a. Bonne journée !   b. Bonne nuit !   (c.) Bonjour !

3. You've been talking to a friend and you want to say "*see you soon*" before going your separate ways. You would say:

    a. Au revoir !   (b.) À bientôt !   c. Salut !

4. You're talking to your boss. You would say:

    a. Je vais bien, merci. Et toi ?   (b.) Je vais bien, merci. Et vous ?

5. How would you answer if somebody asked you, "*Comment ça va?*":

    (a.) Très bien, merci.   b. Salut !   c. Au revoir.

Exercise 1.8 - Translate from French to English and vice versa:

French	English
1. .... Bonjour!	Hello/Hi! (informal)
2. ...... Comment allez-vous?	How are you? (formal)
3. Tout va bien.	...... Everything is good.
4. ...... Salut!	Bye! (informal)
5. Bonne nuit.	...... Good night!
6. Bonne journée.	...... Good day!

Exercise 1.9 - Translate this conversation from French to English:

French	English
Vous: Bonjour Monsieur.Comment allez-vous ?	**You:** _Good day Sir. How are you?_
Votre patron: Bien, merci. Et vous ?	**Your boss:** _Good, thank you. And you?_
Vous: Tout va bien, merci. Au revoir.	**You:** _All is well, thank you. Goodbye._
Votre patron: Bonne journée.	**Your boss:** _Good day._

_100%_

ANSWERS:

Exercise 1.1

Formal discussion (your boss):

Vous (you): Bonjour Monsieur ! *(Hello sir !)*
Votre chef (your boss): Bonjour, comment allez-vous ? *(Hello how are you ?)*
Vous (you): Très bien, merci. Et vous ? *(Very well thank you. And you ?)*
Votre chef (your boss): Très bien, merci. *(Very well thank you.)*

Informal discussion (friends):

Vous (you): Salut ! *(Hi!)*
Votre ami (your friend): Salut XXX, ça va ? *(Hi XXX, how are you?)*
Vous (you): Oui, ça va. Et toi ? *(Yes, I'm fine. And you ?)*
Votre ami (your friend): Pas trop mal, bonne journée. *(Not too bad, have a good day.)*

Exercise 1.2

1/ Comment vas-tu ? 2/ Bonjour ! 3/ Bonne nuit ! 4/Au revoir. 5/Comment allez-vous ?

Exercise 1.3

1/ Good morning! or Hello! 2/Comment ça va ? 3/Bien, merci. 4/Not very well. 5/Et toi ? 6/ Goodbye.

Exercise 1.4 (possible answers)

Vous (you): Bonjour. Comment allez-vous ? *(Hello. How are you ?)*
Votre ami (your friend): Bien, merci. Et vous ? *(Good, thank you. And you ?)*
Vous (you): Bien. Bonne journée. *(Good. Have a good day.)*
Votre ami (your friend): Au revoir. *(Goodbye.)*

Exercise 1.5

1/ Bonsoir. 2/Comment vas-tu ? 3/Very well. 4/ Pas trop mal. 5/Et vous ? 6/See you soon!

Exercise 1.6

Vous: Bonjour. Ça va ?
Votre ami: Pas trop mal. Et toi ?
Vous: Tout va bien. À bientôt !
Votre ami: Salut !

Exercise 1.7

1/ Pas très bien. 2/ Bonne journée ! 3/ À bientôt ! 4/ Je vais bien, merci. Et vous ? 5/ Très bien, merci.

Exercise 1.8

1/ Salut ! 2/ Comment allez-vous ? 3/ Everything is going well. 4/ Salut ! 5/ Good night. 6/ Have a nice day.

Exercise 1.9

You: Good morning, sir. How are you?

Your boss: Well, thank you. And you?

You: Everything is going well, thank you. Goodbye.

Your boss: Have a nice day.

DAY 2
THE ARTICLES

....or how it all begins.

You are already familiar with articles in sentence structures. These are the little words that appear before nouns, announcing their presence, and letting you know beforehand how many there are, and what the gender of the noun is. In English, we don't need to bother with the gender, but that's where it gets interesting in French.

> **Tip:** I suggest that when you start listing nouns for your French vocabulary, you should include the articles on your list. This will make memorizing the gender of the nouns a lot easier.

There are three kinds of articles in French: **definite**, **indefinite**, and **partitive**.

Here's how they differ.

- Definite articles are specific. *(the)*
- Indefinite articles are not. *(a, an, one, some)*
- Partitive articles are used for unknown quantities or uncountable things. *(any, some)*

In English, the definite article is "*the*". Indefinite articles are "*a*" and "*an*" for singular nouns and there is no indefinite article for plural. Partitive articles don't exist in English, but the closest translation would be "*some*" or "*any*".

French articles are more widely used than their English peers.

- "le", "la", "les" (articles définis)

Remember: "**le**" is for masculine singular nouns. "**la**" is for feminine singular nouns. "**les**" is for plural nouns, regardless of whether they are masculine or feminine.

If the noun being presented starts with a vowel or a mute **h, le** or **la** is shortened into **l'**.

Some examples:

[Handwritten margin note, left side, top: "plural use: "des"; Starts w/h + vowel: "de l'"; Fem, singular: masculine + singular: "du"]

[Handwritten margin note, left side: partitive articles: masculine + singular: "du"; feminine singular: "de la"]

[Handwritten margin note, left side, bottom: plural — any gender: "les"; Masculine + singular: "un"; Feminine singular: "une"; Indefinite articles:]

[Handwritten note, bottom center: Definitive articles: If masculine + singular: "le" = the; Feminine + singular: "la" = the]

[Handwritten note, bottom right: plural + any gender: "les"; Singular + starts w/ vowel: "l'"]

10

Track 3

- **le chien** *(the dog)*
- **la reine** *(the queen)*
- **l'ami** *(the friend)*
- **l'homme** *(the man)*
- **le hamster** *(the hamster)*

- **les chiens** *(the dogs)*
- **les reines** *(the queens)*
- **les amis** *(the friends)*
- **les hommes** *(the men)*
- **les hamsters** *(the hamsters)*

Exercise 2.1 - Fill in the blanks with [le], [la], [les] or [l']:

1. __le__ chien de mon voisin est mignon. (*My neighbour's dog is cute.*)

2. __les__ l'ami de mon frère est aussi mon ami. (*My brother's friend is also my friend.*)

3. Passe-moi __l'__ l'eau, s'il te plaît. (*Pass me the water, please.*)

4. __les__ enfants jouent dehors. (*The children are playing outside.*)

5. __la__ maman de mon ami est gentille. (*My friend's mom is nice.*)

- **"un", "une", "des" (articles indéfinis)**

Remember: **"un"** is for masculine singular nouns. **"une"** is for feminine singular nouns. **"des"** is for plural nouns, whether male or female.

Some examples:

Track 4

- **un chien** *(a dog)*
- **une reine** *(a queen)*
- **un ami** *(a friend)*

- **des chiens** *(some/any dogs)*
- **des reines** *(some/any queens)*
- **des amis** *(some/any friends)*

When an indefinite article is used in a negative sentence (ne... pas), **un, une,** and **des** are replaced with **de**. **"De"** changes to **d'** when used with nouns that begin with a vowel or the mute **h**.

- **"du", "de la", "des" (articles partitifs)**

Remember: "du" is for masculine singular nouns. "de la" is for feminine singular nouns. "des" is for plural and doesn't matter if the nouns are masculine or feminine Some or what letter they begin with.

If the noun being presented starts with a vowel or a mute **h, du** or **de la** becomes **de l'** regardless of the gender.

Some examples:

Track 5

- **du gâteau** *(some/any cake)*
  derle =du
- **de la viande** *(some/any meat)*

- **de l'argent (masculine)** *(some/any money)*

- **de l'herbe (feminine)** *(some/any grass)*

- **des gâteaux** *(some/any cakes)*

- **des viandes** *(some/any meats)*

- **des herbes** *(some/any herbs)*

Exercise 2.2 - Fill in the blanks with [un] or [une] or [des]:

1. Je veux adopter __un__ chien. *(I want to adopt a dog.)*
2. J'ai acheté __une__ nouvelle maison. *(I bought a new house.)*
3. Il a acheté __des__ nouvelles chaussures. *(He bought new shoes.)*
4. Elle mange __des__ pommes. *(She's eating apples.)*
5. J'ai trouvé __un__ chat dans la rue. *(I found a cat in the street.)*

LET'S PRACTICE SOME MORE!

Exercise 2.3 - Put the right article in the following exercises:

1. C'est ___un___ chien. *(It is a dog.)*

2. C'est ___une___ fille. *(It is a girl.)*

→ 3. Ce sont ___les___ livres. *(Those are books.)*

4. C'est ___la___ maison de Sophie. *(This is Sophie's house.)*

5. C'est ___le___ livre de Jean. *(It is Jean's book.)*

→ 6. Ce sont ___les___ chocolats de Patrick. *(Those are Patrick's chocolates.)*

> *Fun fact:* The Eiffel Tower is repainted every 7 years.

Exercise 2.4 - Fill the blanks with the correct definite or indefinite article [le / la / l'] or [un / une]:

1. Le Japon, c'est ___le___ pays où ils ont vécu toute leur vie. *(Japan is the country where they made all their lives.)*

2. Est-ce qu'il y a ___un___ bureau de poste dans ce village ? *(Is there a post office in this village?)*

3. À droite, c'est ___la___ chambre des parents. À gauche, ___le___ salon. En face, ___la___ chambre des enfants. Il y a ___une___ salle de bain au premier étage. *(On the right is the parents' room. On the left, the living room. Opposite, the children's room. There is a bathroom on the first floor.)*

4. Tu connais ___la___ mère de Pierre ? *(Do you know Pierre's mother?)*

5. J'habite dans ___la___ rue de l'Amour. *(I live in the rue de l'Amour.)*

6. J'ai stationné ___la___ voiture à la gare. *(I parked the car at the station.)*

7. Voici la clef qui permet d'ouvrir ___la___ chambre. C'est .... numéro 47. *(This is the key that opens the room. It's number 47.)*

8. Nous habitons près de ___la___ place centrale du village. *(We live near the central square of the village.)*

13

9. J'aime beaucoup _le_ soleil, _la_ mer et _le_ sable. (*I love the sun, the sea and the sand.*)

10. Arles, c'est _un_ ville très sympathique. (*Arles is a very nice city.*)

Exercise 2.5 - Put the right articles in the following sentences:

1. C'est _un_ livre. (*It's a book.*)

2. C'est _le_ chocolat. (*It's chocolate.*)

3. C'est _une_ fille. (*It's a girl.*)

4. Ce sont _le_ biscuits. (*Those are biscuits.*)

5. Ce sont _la_ biscuits de Marie. (*Those are Marie's biscuits.*)

Exercise 2.6 - Put these articles in the right column : [le], [un], [des], [les], [une], [de la], [la], [des], and [du]:

Articles définis	Articles indéfinis	Articles partitifs
le, la, (les) l'	un, une, ~~les~~	~~les~~ du, de la, des, de l'

plural

Exercise 2.7 - Put the right articles in the following sentences :

1. Paris est _le_ capitale de la France. (*Paris is the capital of France.*)

2. Jean est _un_ bon garçon. (*Jean is a good boy.*)

3. Je bois _le_ jus d'orange. (*I drink orange juice.*)

4. J'achète _des_ cadeaux pour ma famille. (*I buy gifts for my family.*)

5. Caroline aime _les_ animaux. (*Caroline likes animals.*)

plural.

Exercise 2.8 - Tick the right answer:

1. Il mange _une_ poire. (*He eats a pear.*)

    a. une   b. un   c. la

2. Il prépare _du_ gâteau. (*He's making a cake.*)

    a. le   b. un   c. du

3. J'ai regardé _un_ film au cinéma. (*I watched a movie at the cinema.*)

    a. une   b. des   c. un

4. _Les_ enfants de ma soeur sont gentils. *(My sister's children are nice.)*

    a. des   b. de la   c. les

5. J'ai offert _les_ fleurs à ma maman. *(I offered flowers to my mom.)*

    a. les   b. des   c. une

Exercise 2.9 - Put the right articles in the following sentences :

1. Elle boit _le_ lait. *(She's drinking milk.)*

2. Frank est _le_ meilleur ami de François. *(Frank is François's best friend.)*

3. "_La_ reine des neiges" est un bon film. *("The Snow Queen" is a good movie.)*

4. Il m'a prêté _l'_ argent. *(He lent me money.)*

5. J'ai mangé _du_ gâteau. *(I ate some cake.)*

ANSWERS:

Exercise 2.1

1/ Le 2/ L' 3/ l' 4/ Les 5/ La

Exercise 2.2

1/ un 2/ une 3/ des 4/ des 5/ un

Exercise 2.3

1/ un 2/ une 3/ des 4/ la 5/ le 6/ les

Exercise 2.4

1/ le 2/ un 3/ la ; le ; la ; une 4/ la 5/ la 6/ la 7/ la ; le 8/ la 9/ le ; la ; le 10/ une

Exercise 2.5

Track 6

1/ C'est un livre. 2/ C'est du chocolat. 3/ C'est une fille. 4/ Ce sont des biscuits.
5/ Ce sont les biscuits de Marie.

Exercise 2.6

Articles définis	Articles indéfinis	Articles partitifs
le, la, les	un, une, des	du, de la, des

Exercise 2.7

1/ la 2/ un 3/du 4/ des 5/ les

Exercise 2.8

1/ une 2/ un 3/ un 4/ Les 5/ des

Exercise 2.9

1/ du 2/ le 3/ La 4/ de l' 5/ du

DAY 3
THE VERB "ÊTRE"

..and how this word seems to be popping up everywhere.

One of the most common French verbs you'll be hearing – and using – is **"être"**. It means *"to be"*, and will almost certainly appear frequently in daily speech, expressions, forming other tenses, and indeed, almost everywhere else. In short, you must learn it and make it part of your basic arsenal of French words.

But there's a teeny-tiny bit of bad news: *être* is an *irregular verb*, which basically means it's got rules of its own and there's no predicting the form it's going to take. The best thing to do is to memorize the rules.

The good news? We're handing it to you in spoonfuls. This time, let's take a look at the present tense forms of *être* first.

- If the pronoun being used is **je** for first person singular, you use **suis**. This means *"I am"*.

- If the pronoun is **tu** for second person singular, you use **es**. This means *"you are"*.

- For third person singular pronoun **il** or **elle**, you use **est**. This means *"he/ she is"*.

- For first person plural pronoun **nous**, you use **sommes**. This means *"we are"*.

- For second person plural pronoun **vous**, you use **êtes**. This means *"you are"*.

- For third person plural **ils** or **elles**, you use the form **sont**. This means *"they are"*.

A few examples when used:

Track 7

- Je **suis** heureux. *(I am happy.)*

- Tu **es** heureux. *(You are happy.)*

- Il **est** heureux. *(He is happy.)*

- Nous **sommes** heureux. *(We are happy.)*

- Vous êtes heureux. *(You are happy.)*

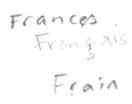

○ Ils **sont** heureux. *(They are happy.)*

See? It's quite easy.

Here's a little chart for guidance, if you're into that kind of thing...

Track 8

Pronoun	"être" form in Present Tense
Je	suis
Tu	es
Il/Elle	est
Nous	sommes
Vous	êtes
Ils/Elles	sont

LET'S PRACTICE !

Exercise 3.1 - Choose the right tense of the verb "*être*" here:

1. Je ___suis___ Français. *(I am French.)*

2. Vous ___êtes___ gentil. *(You are nice.)*

3. Désolé, nous ___sommes___ en retard. *(Sorry, we are late.)*

4. Tu ___es___ grand. *(You are tall.)*

5. Ils ___sont___ énervés. *(They are upset.)*

6. Nous ___sommes___ contents. *(We are happy.)*

> **Fun fact:** French toast and french fries aren't French in origin.

Exercise 3.2 - Tick the correct answer:

1. Je _____ Français. *(I am French.)*
   - a. est
   - b. sommes
   - c. suis ✓

2. Ils _____ mariés. *(They are married.)*
   - a. sont ✓
   - b. est
   - c. sommes

3. Nous _____ contents. *(We are happy.)*
   - a. sont
   - b. sommes ✓
   - c. êtes

4. Vous _____ toujours en retard. *(You are always late.)*
   - a. êtes ✓
   - b. sommes
   - c. sont

5. Tu _____ très gentil. *(You are very nice.)*
   - a. est
   - b. es ✓
   - c. êtes

Exercise 3.3 - Re-order these words to make sentences:

1. suis/Je/content - _Je suis content_
2. belle/es/Tu - _Tu es belle_
3. Elle/méchante/est - _Elle est méchante_
4. Nous/sommes/désolés - _Nous sommes désolés_
5. sont/à l'école/ Ils - _Ils sont à l'école_

Exercise 3.4 - Conjugate the verb "être" in the present tense:

1. Il _est_ un gentil garcon. (*He is a nice kid.*)
2. Nous _sommes_ fiers de toi. (*We are proud of you.*)
3. Vous _êtes_ beaux ensemble. (*You are beautiful together.*)
4. Elles _sont_ soeurs. (*They are sisters.*)
5. Je _suis_ ravi de vous connaître. (*I am delighted to meet you.*)

Exercise 3.5 - Complete this dialogue with the right form of the verb "être":

Paul : Bonjour, est-ce que Marie _est_ là ? (*Hello, is Marie here?*)

La maman de Marie : Non, elle n' _est_ pas là. Elle _est_ chez le docteur avec son papa. Ils _sont_ tous les deux malades. Tu veux lui laisser un message ? Tu veux?

(*No, she's not here. She went to the doctor with her dad. They are both sick. Do you want to leave a message for her? You are ___?*)

Paul : Paul. Je _suis_ Paul. Oui, merci beaucoup. (*Paul. I am Paul. Yes, thank you very much.*)

Exercise 3.6 - Translate these sentences from English to French:

English	French
1. I am French.	Je suis Français.
2. They are happy. (m.)	Ils sont conténtes
3. He is tall.	Il est grande
4. We are late.	Nous sommes an retard
5. You are nice. (pl.)	Ils sont gentiles

Exercise 3.7 - Conjugate the verb "être" in the present tense:

1. Les enfants de ma sœur _Sont_ gentils. *(My sister's kids are nice.)*

2. Les bananes _sont_ mûres. *(The bananas are ripe.)*

3. Le dîner _est_ délicieux. *(The dinner is delicious.)*

4. Ma famille et moi _Sommes_ en vacances. *(My family and I are on vacation.)*

5. Mes vêtements _Sont_ sales. *(My clothes are dirty.)*

Exercise 3.8 - Translate these sentences from French to English:

French	English
1. Ils sont Français.	They are French
2. Elle est grande.	she is tall
3. Je suis content.	I am happy
4. Tu es en retard.	You are late
5. Elles sont gentilles.	They are nice

Exercise 3.9 - Find the mistake in each sentence and rewrite it correctly:

1. Ils est Français. *(They are French.)*   - Ils sont Français

2. Nous sont contents. *(We are happy.)*   - Nous sommes content

3. Elle sont gentille. *(They are nice.)*   - Elle es gentille.

4. Vous es drôles. *(You are funny.)*   - Vous êtes drôles

5. Tu est en retard. *(You are late.)*   - Tu es en retard.

ANSWERS:

Exercise 3.1

Track 9

1/ Je suis Français. *(I am French.)* 2/ Vous êtes gentil. *(You are nice.)* 3/ Désolé, nous sommes en retard. *(Sorry, we are late.)* 4/ Tu es grand. *(You are tall.)* 5/ Ils sont énervés. *(They are upset.)* 6/ Nous sommes contents. *(We are happy.)*

Exercise 3.2

1/ suis 2/ sont 3/ sommes 4/ êtes 5/es

Exercise 3.3

1/ Je suis content. *(I am happy.)* 2/ Tu es belle. *(You are pretty.)* 3/ Elle est méchante. *(She is mean.)* 4/ Nous sommes désolés. *(We are sorry.)* 5/ Ils sont à l'école. *(They are at school.)*

Exercise 3.4

1/ Il est un gentil garcon. 2/ Nous sommes fiers de toi. 3/ Vous êtes beaux ensemble. 4/ Elles sont sœurs. 5/ Je suis ravi de vous connaître.

Exercise 3.5

Paul : Bonjour, est-ce que Marie est là ?
La maman de Marie : Non, elle n'est pas là. Elle est chez le docteur avec son papa. Ils sont tous les deux malades. Tu veux lui laisser un message. Tu es... ?
Paul : Paul. Je suis Paul. Oui, merci beaucoup.

Exercise 3.6

1/ Je suis Français. 2/ Il est grand. 3/ Ils sont contents. 4/ Nous sommes en retard. 5/ Vous êtes gentils.

Exercise 3.7

1/ Les enfants de ma sœur sont gentils. 2/ Les bananes sont mûres. 3/ Le dîner est délicieux. 4/ Ma famille et moi sommes en vacances. 5/ Mes vêtements sont sales.

Exercise 3.8

1/ They are French. 2/ She is tall. 3/ I am happy. 4/ You are late. 5/ They are nice.

Exercise 3.9

1/ Ils sont Français. 2/ Nous sommes contents. 3/ Elle est gentille.
4/ Vous êtes drôles. 5/ Tu es en retard.

...or when no can do.

Negative sentences are quite easy to make. In English, we simply pepper our words with "*not*" or the shortened form "*-n't*". In French, two words are needed to do this: **"ne...pas"**. Other words such as **"jamais"** or **"rien"** (*nothing*) can also take the place of **"pas"** in other instances.

Here are the French negatives.

Track 10

ne...	pas	*not*
ne...	rien	*nothing, not...anything*
ne...	personne	*no one, nobody, not...anyone, not...anybody*
ne...	jamais	*never, not...ever*
ne...	plus	*no more, no longer, not...any longer, not...anymore*

Now for some basics you should take note of:

- When forming negative sentences, the verb is sandwiched in the middle of **"ne"** and **"pas"**.

  Example: Je **ne** <u>parle</u> **pas** français. (*I don't speak French.*)

  Take note that the verb <u>parle</u> is right smack in the middle of the two.

- If the verb being used starts with a vowel, **"ne"** is shortened to **"n"**.

  Example: Je **n'**aime **pas** les frites. (*I don't like fries.*)

- When the sentence contains an object pronoun (these are "*him*", "*her*", or "*it*" in English or **"te"**, **"le"**, or **"lui"** in French), the format changes slightly, and the object pronoun gets included in the middle of the "**ne...pas**" sandwich.

  Here's how it goes: **subject + ne + pronoun + verb + pas**.

  Example: Je **ne** t'entends **pas**. (*I can't hear you.*), where **tu** is shortened to **t'**.

- If the tense you are using contains two verbs such as the perfect tense or pluperfect, this is the format: **ne (n') + avoir or être + pas + past participle**.

  Example: Je **n'**ai **rien** dit. *(I did not say anything.)*

- **"Non plus"** is similar to the English term *"neither"*.

  Example: Moi **non plus**. *(Me neither.)*

- In informal conversations, French speakers no longer include **"ne"** and just jump right in with the rest of the words.

  Example: Il (**ne**) me l'a **pas** dit. *(He did not tell me.)*

- **"Non"** and **"pas"** are used to answer a question negatively. **Non** can mean no or not, while **pas** is used in a more emphatic way.

  Example: **Pas** moi! *(Not me!)* or **Pas** question ! *(No way!)*

LET'S PRACTICE!

Exercise 4.1 - Choose the right answer:

1. *He doesn't have a laptop.*

    a. Il n'a plus d'ordinateur portable.

    b. Il n'a pas d'ordinateur portable.

    c. Il n'a jamais d'ordinateur portable.

2. *They didn't sing. Me neither.*

    a. Elles n'ont pas chanté. Moi, non plus.

    b. Elles n'ont rien chanté. Moi, non plus.

    c. Elles n'ont plus chanté. Moi, non plus.

3. *I don't want to go (there).*

    a. Je ne veux jamais y aller.

    b. Je ne veux jamais plus y aller.

    c. Je ne veux pas y aller.

4. *We aren't ever going.*

    a. On n'a qu'à y aller.

    b. On n'y va.

    c. On n'y va jamais.

5. *You aren't in New York anymore.*

    a. Je ne suis plus à New York

    b. Tu n'es plus à New York.

    c. Tu n'es pas à New York.

6. *We won't ever see it anymore.*

    a. On ne le verra plus jamais.

    b. On ne le verra jamais.

    c. On ne le verra plus.

7. *We have nothing to lose.*

    a. On n'a qu'à perdre.

    b. On a tout à perdre.

    c. On n'a rien à perdre.

8. *We have nothing to lose anymore.*

    a. On n'a plus rien à perdre.

    b. On n'a plus à perdre.

    c. On n'a rien à perdre.

9. *You aren't kind.*

    a. Vous n'êtes ni intelligent ni gentil.

    b. Vous n'êtes jamais gentil.

    c. Vous n'êtes pas gentil.

10. *We haven't seen anybody.*

    a. Nous n'avons plus vu personne.

    b. Nous avons vu une personne.

    c. Nous n'avons vu personne.

Fun fact: It's against the law in France to take pictures of police officers and police vehicles.

Exercise 4.2 - Choose the right translation for each sentence:

1. *I don't like cheese.*

    a. Je n'aime pas le fromage.

    b. Je n'aime plus le fromage.

    c. Je n'ai jamais aimé le fromage.

2. *I have never been to Japan.*

    a. Je ne suis pas allé au Japon.

    b. Je ne suis jamais allé au Japon.

    c. Je voudrais aller au Japon.

3. *We have nothing to lose.*

    a. On n'a rien à perdre.

    b. On a tout à perdre.

    c. On n'a jamais perdu.

4. *I don't like you anymore.*

    a. Je ne t'aime pas.

    b. Je ne t'ai jamais aimé.

    c. Je ne t'aime plus.

5. *I don't see anyone.*

    a. Je ne vois personne.

    b. Je ne vois pas une personne.

    c. Je ne vois plus de personne.

Exercise 4.3 - Transform these affirmative sentences to negative ones:

1. J'aime les pommes. *(I like apples.)*   -_____

2. Il fait du sport. *(He plays sports.)*   -_____

3. Ils sont mariés. *(They are married.)*   -_____

4. La robe est rouge. *(The dress is red.)*   -_____

5. Elle travaille ici. *(She works here.)*   -_____

Exercise 4.4 - Transform these negative sentences to affirmative ones:

1. Cette jupe n'est pas verte. *(This skirt is not green.)*

_____

2. Ce film n'est pas mauvais. *(This movie is not bad.)*

_____

3. Ils ne sont pas méchants. *(They are not mean.)*

_____

4. Ce travail n'est pas difficile. *(This work is not hard.)*

_____

5. Je ne suis pas fatigué. *(I am not tired.)*

_____

Exercise 4.5 - Choose the right translation for these sentences:

1. Il n'a jamais conduit.

    a. He always drove.

    b. He never drove.

    c. He doesn't drive.

2. Elle ne travaille plus.

    a. She's always working.

    b. She doesn't work.

    c. She doesn't work anymore.

3. Je ne connais personne ici.

    a. I know everybody here.

    b. I don't know anybody here.

    c. I don't know anybody anymore.

4. Je n'ai pas assez d'argent pour acheter une maison.

    a. I don't have enough money to buy a house.

    b. I have enough money to buy a house.

    c. I don't have enough money to buy a house anymore.

5. Je n'ai rien à te donner.

    a. I have nothing to give you.

    b. I have nothing to give you anymore.

    c. I have something to give you.

Exercise 4.6 - Transform these affirmative sentences to negative ones:

1. Je t'aime toujours. *(I still love you.)*

    _____

2. La maison est grande. *(The house is big.)*

    _____

3. La fenêtre est ouverte. *(The window is open.)*

_____

4. Je comprends tout. *(I understand everything.)*

_____

5. Je parle français. *(I speak French.)*

_____

Exercise 4.7 - Choose the right answer:

1. "Je n'aime pas les olives." "Moi non plus." What does "moi non plus" mean here?

    a. Me neither.

    b. I don't.

    c. Me too.

2. Which one of these is said in an informal conversation?

    a. Je n'aime plus les fraises.

    b. J'aime pas les fraises.

    c. Je n'aime pas les fraises.

3. "Qui a cassé ce vase ? " "Pas moi ! ". What does "pas moi" mean here?

    a. Me!

    b. Not me!

    c. Him!

4. "Maman, est-ce que je peux sortir ce soir ? " "Pas question ! ". What doe "pas question" mean here?

    a. No way!

    b. Don't!

    c. No question!

Exercise 4.8 - Transform these affirmative sentences to negative ones:

1. Je t'entends. *(I hear you.)*

   _____

2. Il lui a donné de l'argent. *(He gave him/her money.)*

   _____

3. Je l'ai vu hier. *(I saw him yesterday.)*

   _____

4. Elle lui demande son numéro de téléphone. *(She asks him for his phone number.)*

   _____

5. Je lui parle en français. *(I talk to him in French.)*

   _____

Exercise 4.9 - Complete these sentences with [pas], [plus], [rien], [personne] ou [jamais] :

1. J'aimais ce film avant. Maintenant, je ne l'aime _____. *(I liked this movie before. Now, I don't like it anymore.)*

2. J'aimerais bien voyager. Je ne l'ai _____ fait. *(I would like to travel. I've never done it.)*

3. Je n'ai _____ fait de toute la journée. *(I've done nothing all day long.)*

4. Où sont les gens ? Je ne vois _____ ici. *(Where are the people? I don't see anyone here.)*

5. Hier, j'ai fait la vaisselle. Aujourd'hui, je ne l'ai _____ faite. *(Yesterday, I washed the dishes. Today, I didn't do it.)*

ANSWERS:

Exercise 4.1

Track 11

1/ B. Il n'a pas d'ordinateur portable. 2/ A. Elles n'ont pas chanté. Moi, non plus.
3/ C. Je ne veux pas y aller. 4/ C. On n'y va jamais. 5/ B. Tu n'es plus à New York.
6/ A. On ne le verra plus jamais. 7/ C. On n'a rien à perdre. 8/ A. On n'a plus rien
à perdre. 9/ C. Vous n'êtes pas gentil. 10/ C. Nous n'avons vu personne

Exercise 4.2

1/ Je n'aime pas le fromage. 2/ Je ne suis jamais allé au Japon. 3/ On n'a rien à
perdre. 4/ Je ne t'aime plus. 5/ Je ne vois personne.

Exercise 4.3

1/ Je n'aime pas les pommes. 2/ Il ne fait pas de sport. 3/ Ils ne sont pas mariés.
4/ La robe n'est pas rouge. 5/ Elle ne travaille pas ici.

Exercise 4.4

1/ Cette jupe est verte. 2/ Ce film est mauvais. 3/ Ils sont méchants.
4/ Ce travail est difficile. 5/ Je suis fatigué.

Exercise 4.5

1/ He never drove. 2/ She doesn't work anymore. 3/ I don't know anybody here.
4/ I don't have enough money to buy a house. 5/ I have nothing to give you.

Exercise 4.6

1/ Je ne t'aime plus. 2/ La maison n'est pas grande. 3/ La fenêtre n'est pas ouverte.
4/ Je ne comprends rien. 5/ Je ne parle pas français.

Exercise 4.7

1/ Me neither. 2/ J'aime pas les fraises. 3/ not me 4/ No way!

Exercise 4.8

1/ Je ne t'entends pas. 2/ Il ne lui a pas donné d'argent. 3/ Je ne l'ai pas vu hier.
4/ Elle ne lui demande pas son numéro de téléphone. 5/ Je ne lui parle pas en
français.

Exercise 4.9

1/ plus 2/ jamais 3/ rien 4/ personne 5/ pas

DAY 5
THERE IS

...there are a bunch of uses for this.

One of the most common expressions you'll come across in French is **"il y a"** which means *"there is"* or *"there are"*.

Pronounced as *"ee lya"*, it can appear in basic statements, questions, negative sentences, and other tenses. In short, you'll find that it is basically all over the place.

Using **"il y a"** is a quick and easy way to say a lot of things in a simple format. This is why you should take this time to familiarize yourself with its different permutations and uses.

Here are some important things to remember about "il y a":

- It is composed of these three words:

    - **il** - which more or less means *"it"* in English,

    - **y** - meaning *"there"*

    - **a** - the third person singular form of the verb avoir which means *"to have"*

    Its literal translation means *"it has there"*.

- It usually follows these patterns:

    (1) il y a + indefinite article + noun,

    (2) il y a + number + noun,

    (3) il y a + indefinite pronoun.

    For example: Il y a un chien. *(There is a dog.)*

- It can be used with both singular and plural nouns. Just like this:
  Il y a deux chiens. *(There are two dogs.)*

- It can be used to ask a question using the **"est-ce que"** format.

    Est-ce qu'il y a un chien ? *(Is there a dog?)*

- It can also be used to ask a question using inversion. Such as this:

    Y a-t-il un chien ? *(Is there a dog?)*

- You can use question words with it too!

  Pourquoi est-ce qu'il y a un chien ? *(Why is there a dog?)*

- It could appear in this format too:

  Qu'est-ce qu'il y a ? This can be loosely translated to *"What is it?"*

- When you want to use it in a negative sentence, you simply change it to **"il n'y a pas"** and change the indefinite article to **"de"**. For example:
  Il n'y a pas de chien. *(There is no dog.)*

- If you want to use **"il y a"** in a different tense, you need to conjugate the verb **"avoir"** to match the tense you are going to use. Some examples:

  Il y avait un chien. *(There was a dog.)*

  Il y aura des chiens. *(There will be some dogs).*

LET'S PRACTICE!

Exercise 5.1

I. Answer these questions by using "il y a" :

1. Dans la cuisine, il y a un four ? *(Is there an oven in the kitchen?)*

   _____

2. Dans votre salon, il y a une table et un canapé ? *(In your living room, is there a table and a sofa?)*

   _____

3. Dans votre chambre, il y a un grand lit ou un petit lit? *(Is there a double bed or a small bed in your room?)*

   _____

4. Dans la salle de bain, il y a une douche ou une baignoire ? *(Is there a shower or a tub in the bathroom?)*

   _____

II. Exercise 5.1.2 - Form some sentences similar to the example below :

Ex̲ample: Chine/pandas. → En Chine, il y a des pandas. *(In China, there are pandas.)*

1. Japon/girafes *(Japan/giraffes)*

   _____

2. Paris/Tour Eiffel *(Paris/Eiffel Tower)*

   _____

3. Londres/la statue de la Liberté *(London/Statue of Liberty)*

   _____

4. Australie/kangourous *(Australia/kangaroos)*

   _____

> **Fun fact:** The French had an early version of the internet called Minitel as long ago as 1984. They could pay bills and shop at home using the Minitel service.

Exercise 5.2
Create sentences similar to the example below:

Example: fleurs/jardin. ➜ Dans le jardin, il y a des fleurs. *(In the garden, there are flowers.)*

1. nuages/ciel. *(clouds/sky)*

   _____

2. élèves/école. *(pupils/school)*

   _____

3. jouets/chambre d'enfant. *(toys/kid's room)*

   _____

4. tables/salle de classe. *(tables/classroom)*

   _____

5. vêtements/machine à laver. *(clothes/washing machine)*

   _____

Exercise 5.3 - Transform these affirmative sentences to negative ones:

Example: Il y a un chien. *(There is a dog)* ➜ Il n'y a pas de chien. *(There is no dog.)*

1. Il y a un miroir dans le salon. *(There is a mirror in the living room.)*

   _____

2. Il y a du lait dans le réfrigérateur. *(There is milk in the fridge.)*

   _____

3. Il y a des oiseaux dans le ciel. *(There are birds in the sky.)*

   _____

4. Il y a des voitures dans le parking. *(There are cars in the parking lot.)*

   _____

5. Il y a un crayon dans ma trousse. *(There is a pencil in my pencil case.)*

   _____

Exercise 5.4 - Create questions using the est-ce que format (see the example below):

Example: un chien/jardin. ➔ Est ce qu'il y a un chien dans le jardin ? *(Is there a dog in the garden?)*

1. une chambre libre/hôtel. *(a free room/hotel)*

   _____

2. du sucre/café. *(sugar/coffee)*

   _____

3. des cours de danse/salle de gym. *(dance classes/gym)*

   _____

4. un lion/zoo. *(a lion/zoo)*

   _____

5. des toilettes/ici. *(toilets/here)*

   _____

Exercise 5.5 - Create questions using inversions (see the example below):

Example: Il y a un chien. ➔ Y a-t-il un chien ? *(Is there a dog?)*

1. Il y a un concert. *(There is a concert.)*

   _____

2. Il y a un climatiseur dans la chambre. *(There is an air conditioner in the room.)*

   _____

3. Il y a un balcon dans cet appartement. *(There is a balcony in this apartment.)*

   _____

4. Il y a une banque près d'ici. *(There is a bank near here.)*

   _____

5. Il y a des taxis par ici. *(There are taxis here.)*

   _____

ANSWERS:

Exercise 5.1

Track 12

I. 1/ Oui, dans la cuisine, il y a un four. 2/ Oui, il y a une table et un canapé. 3/ Il y a un petit lit 4/ Il y a une douche

II. 1/ Il n'y a pas de girafes au Japon. 2/ Il y a la tour Eiffel à Paris. 3/ Il n'y a pas la statue de la Liberté à Londres 4. En Australie, il y a des kangourous.

Exercise 5.2

1/ Dans le ciel, il y a des nuages. 2/ Dans l'école, il y a des élèves. 3/ Dans la chambre d'enfant, il y a des jouets. 4/ Dans la salle de classe, il y a des tables. 5/ Dans la machine à laver, il y a des vêtements.

Exercise 5.3

1/ Il n'y a pas de miroir dans le salon. 2/ Il n'y a pas de lait dans le réfrigérateur. 3/ Il n'y a pas d'oiseau dans le ciel. 4/ Il n'y a pas de voiture dans le parking. 5/ Il n'y a pas de crayon dans ma trousse.

Exercise 5.4

1/ Est-ce qu'il y a une chambre libre dans l'hôtel ? 2/ Est-ce qu'il y a du sucre dans le café ? 3/ Est-ce qu'il y a des cours de danse dans la salle de gym ? 4/ Est-ce qu'il y a un lion dans le zoo ? 5/ Est-ce qu'il y a des toilettes ici ?

Exercise 5.5

1/ Y a-t-il un concert ? 2/ Y a-t-il un climatiseur dans la chambre ?
3/ Y a-t-il un balcon dans cet appartement ? 4/ Y a-t-il une banque près d'ici ?
5/ Y a-t-il des taxis près d'ici ?

DAY 6
ASKING QUESTIONS

There are not one, not two, but five different ways to ask questions in French. From the very simple to the downright complicated, you may take your pick. But before you get the opportunity, you should be familiar with all of them first.

1. Turning a statement into a question

This is by far the easiest because all you have to do to change any statement into a question is change the pitch of your voice. In writing, just add a question mark at the end and you're all set.

Take these examples:

Track 13

> o **C'est vrai.** *(That's true.)*
>
> o **C'est vrai ?** *(Is that true?)*
>
> o **Vous aimez la France.** *(You like France.)*
>
> o **Vous aimez la France ?** *(Do you like France?)*

2. Using "est-ce que"

Another way is to add **"est-ce que"** to the beginning of a sentence. It literally means *"is it that"* in English, and inserting it before a regular statement can turn it into a question. The rest of the sentence structure stays the same. Easy enough?

Track 14

For example:

> o **Est-ce qu'il est arrivé ?** *(Has he arrived?)*

Exercise 6.1 - Change these statements into questions using "est-ce que":

1. Vous aimez la France. *(You like France.)*

   _____

2. C'est votre chien. *(It's your dog.)*

   _____

3. Vous parlez le français. *(You speak French.)*

_____

4. Il est un bon ami. *(He's a good friend.)*

_____

5. Elle est arrivée. *(She arrived.)*

_____

3. Changing the order of the words to form a question (inversion)

This is the formal way of asking questions in French, and all you need to do is move the sentence structure around a bit. Normally, the subject is followed by the verb, but for the inverted questions, the verb is placed before the subject and then joined by a hyphen.

Example:

Track 15

o **Vous aimez la France.** *(You like France.)*

o **Aimez-vous la France ?** *(Do you like France?)*

Exercise 6.2 - Change these statements by changing the order of the words :

1. Vous aimez la France. *(You like France.)*

_____

2. C'est votre chien. *(It's your dog.)*

_____

3. Vous parlez le français. *(You speak French.)*

_____

4. Il est un bon ami. *(He's a good friend.)*

_____

5. Elle est arrivée. *(She arrived.)*

_____

4. USING N'EST-CE PAS PAS OR NON

If you're confident that the person you are talking to agrees with you, you can add **"n'est-ce pas"** at the end of the sentence. It is just similar to the English usage of *"isn't it?"* or *"right?"* at the end of a question.

"Non" works the same way. It literally means *"no"* and is also added at the end of the sentence. Another one is **"hein"**. It is just like saying *"eh?"* in English, and is often used in informal conversation.

Some examples:

Track 16

- **Vous aimez la France, n'est-ce pas ?** *(You like France, don't you?)*
- **Il est arrivé, n'est-ce pas ?** *(He arrived, didn't he?)*
- **Vous aimez la France, non ?** *(You like France, right?)*
- **Vous aimez la France, hein ?** *(You like France, eh?)*

Exercise 6.3 - Change these statements into questions using "n'est-ce pas" or "non":

1. Il fait du sport. *(He plays sports.)*

   _____

2. Elle est à la maison. *(She's at home.)*

   _____

3. Tu as lavé la vaisselle. *(You cleaned the dishes.)*

   _____

4. Tu aimes le vin. *(You like wine.)*

   _____

5. Ils sont ensemble. *(They are together.)*

   _____

5. Using question words

Last, but definitely not the easiest, is to use interrogative words. The question words may be placed at the start or end of the sentence. It can also appear right before *est-ce que*, or before the inverted subject and verb.

Example: *When did you arrive?*

Track 17

- **Quand est-ce que tu es arrivé ?**
- **Quand es-tu arrivé ?**
- **Quand t'es arrivé ?**
- **T'es arrivé quand ?**

The commonly used question words:

combien + verb ? **combien de + noun ?**	*How much?, how many?* *How much?, how many?*
comment ?	*How?*
où ?	*Where?*
pourquoi ?	*Why?*
quand ?	*When?*
qui, que or quoi ?	*Who, whom, or what?* (depending on the usage)
quel, quels, quelle, or quelles ?	*Who, which, or what?* (depending on how it's used)
lequel, laquelle, lesquels or lesquelles ?	*Which one?* (these are different forms of "lequel" based on gender and count)

Exercise 6.4 - Complete these questions with the right question words :

1. _____ coûte ce téléphone ? (__ *this phone cost?*)

2. _____ frères et soeurs avez-vous ? (__ *brothers and sisters do you have?*)

3. _____ sont mes nouvelles chaussures ? (__ *are my new shoes?*)

4. _____ faire pour aller à la gare ? (__ *do I get to the train station?*)

5. _____ aimes-tu les chiens ? (__ *do you like dogs?*)

Exercise 6.5 - Complete these questions with the right question words :

1. _____ les cours commencent-ils ? (__ *do classes begin?*)

2. _____ d'entre vous est médecin ? (__ *of you is a doctor?*)

3. _____ est le président de la France ? (__ *is the president of France?*)

4. _____ est ton film préféré ? (__ *is your favourite movie?*)

5. _____ veut dire " salut " en français ? (__ *does "salut" mean in French?*)

LET'S PRACTICE SOME MORE!

Exercise 6.6 - Fill in the blanks with the correct answer :

1. (Elle aide) _____ Corinne à faire ses devoirs ? *(Does she help Corinne with her homework?)*

   Aide-elle ? / Aide-t elle ? / Aide t-elle ? / Aide-t-elle ?

2. (Vois-tu) _____ Paul ? *(Can you see Paul?)*

   Est ce que tu vois ? / Est-ce que tu vois ? / Estce que tu vois ? / Est-que tu vois ?

3. (Que fait-il) _____ ce week-end ? *(What's he doing this weekend?)*

   Q'est-ce qu'il fait ? / Qu'est-ce qu'il fait ? / Qu'estce-qu'il fait ? / Quesqu'il fait ?

4. (What) ____ veux-tu pour Noël ? *(What do you want for Christmas?)*

   Que ? / Quand ? / Qu' ? / Qui ?

5. (Vous avez écouté) _____la radio hier soir ? *(Did you listen to the radio last night?)*

   Avez-vous écouté ? / Avez vous écouté ? / Avezvous écouté ? / Vous-avez écouté ?

6. (Aime-t-elle) _____ les chats ? *(Does she like cats?)*

   Est-ce-qu'elle aime ? / Est ce qu'elle aime ? / Estc'est elle aime ? / Est-ce qu'elle aime ?

7. (Who) ____ as-tu rencontré au supermarché ? *(Who did you meet in the supermarket?)*

   Quand ? / Qu' ? / Que ? / Qui ?

8. (Vous étudiez) _____ l'anglais depuis longtemps ? *(Have you been learning English for a long time?)*

   Étudiez-vous ? / Vous étudiez-vous ? / Étudiez-tvous ? / Étudiez vous ?

9. (Vont-ils) _____ en France cette année ? *(Are they going to France this year?)*

    Est ce qu'ils vont ? / Est-qu'ils vont ? / Est-ce qu'ils vont ? / Est-ce-qu'ils vont ?

10. (Tu sais) _____ jouer de la guitare ? *(Can you play the guitar?)*

    Tu-sais ? / Tu sais ? / Sais-tu ? / Sais tu ?

> ***Fun fact:*** It's illegal to kiss on railways in France (oops).

Exercise 6.7 - Choose the correct answer :

1. You want to ask somebody his/her name. You should say:

    a. Comment t'appelles-tu ? (informal)/ Comment vous appelez-vous ? (formal)

    b. Qui es-tu ? (informal)/ Qui êtes-vous ? (formal)

    c. Qui t'appelles tu ? (informal)/ Qui vous appelez-vous ? (formal)

2. You want to ask somebody his/her age. You should say:

    a. Quand est ton âge ? / Quand est votre âge ?

    b. Quel âge as-tu ?/ Quel âge avez-vous ?

    c. Combien est ton âge ? / Combien est votre âge ?

3. You want to know where the toilets are. You should say:

    a. Y a-t-il des toilettes ?

    b. Où sont les toilettes ?

    c. Combien y a-t-il de toilettes ?

4. You want to know when the train arrives. You should say:

    a. Où est le train ?

    b. Quel est le train pour Paris ?

    c. Quand est-ce que le train arrive ?

Exercise 6.8 - Choose the correct translation :

1. *What are you doing this weekend?*

    a. Que fait-il ce week-end ?

    b. Que fais-tu ce week-end ?

    c. Quand est le week-end ?

2. *When are you coming ?*

    a. D'où est-ce que vous venez ?

    b. Quand venez-vous ?

    c. Comment venez-vous ?

3. *Where do you live?*

    a. Où est-ce que vous habitez ?

    b. Qui habite avec vous ?

    c. Pourquoi habitez-vous ici ?

4. *Do you have a brother or a sister?*

    a. Combien as-tu de frères et sœurs ?

    b. As-tu un frère ou une sœur ?

    c. Où sont tes frères et sœurs ?

5. *Which one of them is your dog?*

    a. Où est ton chien ?

    b. Comment va ton chien ?

    c. Lequel d'entre eux est ton chien ?

Exercise 6.9 - Choose the correct translation :

1. *Do you like cats?*

   a. Quel chat aimes-tu ?

   b. Pourquoi aimes-tu les chats ?

   c. Aimes-tu les chats ?

2. *Where is he?*

   a. Où est-il ?

   b. Quand est-ce qu'il arrive ?

   c. Qui est-il ?

3. *Did you eat lunch today?*

   a. Avez-vous déjeuné aujourd'hui ?

   b. Voudrais-tu déjeuner aujourd'hui ?

   c. Quand est-ce que tu as déjeuné aujourd'hui ?

4. *Who sings this song?*

   a. Qui chante cette chanson ?

   b. Qui chantait cette chanson ?

   c. Où se chante cette chanson ?

5. *Which one of you is Marie?*

   a. Lequel d'entre vous est Marie ?

   b. Laquelle d'entre vous est Marie ?

   c. Qui est Marie ?

ANSWERS:

Exercise 6.1

1/ Est-ce que vous aimez la France ? 2/ Est-ce que c'est votre chien ?
3/ Est-ce que vous parlez le français ? 4/ Est-ce qu'il est un bon ami ?
5/ Est-ce qu'elle est arrivée ?

Exercise 6.2

1/ Aimez-vous la France ? 2/ Est-ce votre chien ? 3/ Parlez-vous le français ?
4/ Est-il un bon ami ? 5/ Est-elle arrivée ?

Exercise 6.3

1/ Il fait du sport, n'est-ce pas ? 2/ Elle est à la maison, non ?
3/ Tu as lavé la vaisselle, n'est-ce pas ? 4/ Tu aimes le vin, n'est-ce pas ?
5/ Ils sont ensemble, non ?

Exercise 6.4

1/ Combien coûte ce téléphone ? 2/ Combien de frères et sœurs avez-vous ?
3/ Où sont mes nouvelles chaussures ? 4/ Comment faire pour aller à la gare ?
5/ Pourquoi aimes-tu les chiens ?

Exercise 6.5

1/ Quand les cours commencent-ils ? 2/ Lequel d'entre vous est médecin ?
3/ Qui est le président de la France ? 4/ Quel est ton film préféré ?
5/ Que veut dire "salut" en français ?

Exercise 6.6
Track 18

1/ Aide-t elle Corinne à faire ses devoirs ? 2/ Est-ce que tu vois Paul ?
3/ Qu'est-ce qu'il fait ce week-end ? 4/ Que veux-tu pour Noël ?
5/ Avez-vous écouté la radio hier soir ? 6/ Est-ce-qu'elle aime les chats ?
7/ Qui as-tu rencontré au supermarché ? 8/ Étudiez-vous l'anglais depuis longtemps
? 9/ Est-ce qu'ils vont en France cette année ? 10/ Sais-tu jouer de la guitare ?

Exercise 6.7

1/ Comment t'appelles-tu ? (informal)/ Comment vous appelez-vous ? (formal)

2/ Quel âge as-tu ?/ Quel âge avez-vous ? 3/ Où sont les toilettes ?
4/ Quand est-ce que le train arrive ?

Exercise 6.8

1/ Que fais-tu ce week-end ? 2/ Quand venez-vous ? 3/ Où est-ce que vous habitez ?
4/ As-tu un frère ou une sœur ? 5/ Lequel d'entre eux est ton chien ?

Exercise 6.9

1/ Aimes-tu les chats ? 2/ Où est-il ? 3/ Avez-vous déjeuné aujourd'hui ?
4/ Qui chante cette chanson ? 5/ Laquelle d'entre vous est Marie ?

DAY 7
SIMPLE PRESENT

When we talk about a current action, something that is true in the moment, habitual events, or widely accepted truths, we use the simple present tense.

Regular verbs generally fall into one of three categories based on the verb endings: **"-er"**, **"-ir"**, and **"-re"**. To conjugate these verbs, you have to take note of the applicable rules for each type.

Ready? Let's start with the "-er" verbs.

To form the present tense for the *-er* verbs, use the infinitive, chop off the *-er* and add the new ending which depends on the subject of the sentence.

For example, the verb **donner** is changed to its stem **donn** + the new ending.

Track 19

- For first-person singular, add the new ending **"-e"**.

  Example: **Je donne** *(I give)*

- For second-person singular, add **"-es"**.

  Example: **Tu donnes** *(You give)*

- For third-person singular, add **"-e"**.

  Example: **Il/Elle donne** *(He/she gives)*

- For first-person plural, add **"-ons"**.

  Example: **Nous donnons** *(We give)*

- For second-person plural, add **"-ez"**.

  Example: **Vous donnez** *(You give)*

- For third-person plural, add **"-ent"**.

  Example: **Ils/Elles donnent** *(They give)*

Exercise 7.1 - Conjugate the verbs in brackets in the simple present tense:

1. Je (aimer) _____ énormément ce film. *(I really like this movie.)*

2. Ils (travailler) _____ jour et nuit. *(They work day and night.)*

3. Elle (parler) _____ très bien le français. *(She speaks French very well.)*

4. Nous (manger) _____ dehors ce soir. *(We are eating out tonight.)*

5. Vous (payer) _____ en espèces ou par carte de crédit ? *(Are you going to pay in cash or by credit card?)*

Now for the "-ir" verbs.

To form the present tense for the *-ir* verbs, use the infinitive, chop off the *-ir* and add the new ending.

For example, the verb **finir** is changed to its stem **fin** + the new ending.

Track 20

- For first-person singular, add **"-is"**.

  Example: **Je finis** *(I finish)*

- For second-person singular, add **"-is"**.

  Example: **Tu finis** *(You finish)*

- For third-person singular, add **"-it"**.

  Example: **Il/Elle finit** *(He/she finishes)*

- For first-person plural, add **"-issons"**.

  Example: **Nous finissons** *(We finish)*

- For second-person plural, add **"-issez"**.

  Example: **Vous finissez** *(You finish)*

- For third-person plural, add **"-issent"**.

  Example: **Ils/Elles finissent** *(They finish)*

Finally, for the "-re" verbs

Track 21

To form the present tense for the *-re* verbs, use the infinitive, chop off the *-re* and add the new ending.

For example, the verb **prendre** is changed to its stem **prend** + the new ending.

- For first-person singular, add **"-s"**.

  Example: **Je prends** *(I take)*

- For second-person singular, add **"-s"**.

  Example: **Tu prends** *(You take)*

- For third-person singular, don't add anything.

  Example: **Il/Elle prend** *(He/she takes)*

- For first-person plural, add **"-ons"**.

  Example: **Nous prenons** *(We take)*

- For second-person plural, add **"-ez"**.

  Example: **Vous prenez** *(You take)*

- For third-person plural, add **"-ent"**.

  Example: **Ils/Elles prennent** *(They take)*

Track 22

Another example:

- For first-person singular, add **"-s"**.

  Example: **J'attends** *(I wait)*

- For second-person singular, add **"-s"**.

  Example: **Tu attends** *(You wait)*

- For third-person singular, don't add anything.

  Example: **Il/Elle attend** *(He/she waits)*

- For first-person plural, add **"-ons"**.

  Example: **Nous attendons** *(We wait)*

- For second-person plural, add **"-ez"**.

  Example: **Vous attendez** *(You wait)*

- For third-person plural, add **"-ent"**.

  Example: **Ils/Elles attendent** *(They wait)*

LET'S PRACTICE!

Exercise 7.2 - Fill in the blanks with the correct answer:

1. Il (écouter) _____ beaucoup la radio. *(He listens to the radio a lot.)*

2. Nous (aimer) _____ ce film. *(We like this film.)*

3. Elle (travailler) _____ à Paris. *(She works in Paris.)*

4. Les enfants (grandir) _____ très vite. *(The children are growing up fast).*

5. Il (vendre) _____ sa voiture. *(He's selling his car.)*

6. Elle (parler) _____ couramment le français. *(She speaks French fluently.)*

7. Nous ne (vendre) _____ pas de chaussures. *(We don't sell shoes.)*

8. Tu ne (répondre) _____ pas à ma question. *(You're not answering my question.)*

> ***Fun fact:*** French is the official language of the United Nations.

Exercise 7.3 - Change the following sentences into plural:

1. Il mange du gâteau. *(He eats cake.)*

   _____

2. J'adore la musique. *(I adore music.)*

   _____

3. Tu danses très bien. *(You dance very well.)*

   _____

4. Elle joue aux cartes. *(She plays cards.)*

   _____

5. Je cherche les toilettes. *(I'm looking for the toilets.)*

   _____

Exercise 7.4 - Conjugate the verbs in brackets in the simple present tense:

1. Elle (finir) _____ ses devoirs avant de jouer. *(She finishes her homework before playing.)*

2. Nous (réfléchir) _____ à une solution. *(We are thinking about a solution.)*

3. Je (rougir) _____ quand je le vois. *(I blush when I see him.)*

4. Vous (choisir) _____ quelle option ? *(Which option do you choose?)*

5. Ils (applaudir) _____ quand le spectacle est fini. *(They applaud when the show is over.)*

Exercise 7.5 - Change the following sentences into singular:

1. Nous choisissons de partir en vacances. *(We choose to go on vacation.)*

   _____

2. Elles réussissent à finir l'examen à temps. *(They succeed in finishing the exam in time.)*

   _____

3. Ils grandissent vite. *(They grow up so fast.)*

   _____

4. Vous réfléchissez trop. *(You think a lot.)*

   _____

5. Ils n'obéissent pas aux ordres. *(They don't obey orders.)*

   _____

Exercise 7.6 - Conjugate the verbs in brackets in the simple present tense:

1. Nous (attendre) _____ le résultat depuis ce matin. *(We've been waiting for the results since this morning.)*

2. Je (prendre) _____ quelle route pour aller au supermarché ? *(Which road do I take to go to the supermarket?)*

3. Ils (vendre) _____ de beaux vêtements. *(They sell beautiful clothes.)*

4. Elle (répondre) _____ au téléphone rapidement. *(She answers the phone quickly.)*

5. Vous (descendre) _____ ici ? *(Are you coming down here?)*

Exercise 7.7 - Change the following sentences from singular into plural, or from plural into singular:

1. J'attends depuis longtemps. *(I've been waiting a long time.)*

   _____

2. Nous rendons visite à notre grand-mère. *(We visit our grandmother.)*

   _____

3. Il entend un bruit étrange venant de dehors. *(He hears a weird sound coming from outside.)*

   _____

4. Répondez aux questions. *(Answer the questions.)*

   _____

5. Je perds toujours mes clés. *(I always lose my keys.)*

   _____

Exercise 7.8 - Conjugate the verbs in brackets in the simple present tense:

1. Il (parler) _____ bien l'anglais. *(He speaks English well.)*

2. Elles (répondre) _____ à toutes les questions. *(They answer all the questions.)*

3. Nous (choisir) _____ de dormir à l'hôtel ce soir. *(We choose to sleep at the hotel tonight.)*

4. J'(attendre) _____ le métro. *(I'm waiting for the metro.)*

5. Vous (marcher) _____ assez vite. *(You walk fast enough.)*

ANSWERS:

Exercise 7.1

1/ J'aime énormément ce film. 2/ Ils travaillent jour et nuit. 3/ Elle parle très bien le français. 4/ Nous mangeons dehors ce soir. 5/ Vous payez en espèces ou par carte de crédit ?

Exercise 7.2
Track 23

1/ Il écoute beaucoup la radio. 2/ Nous aimons ce film. 3/ Elle travaille à Paris. 4/ Les enfants grandissent très vite. 5/ Il vend sa voiture. 6/ Elle parle couramment le francais. 7/ Nous ne vendons pas de chaussures. 8/ Tu ne réponds pas à ma question.

Exercise 7.3

1/ Ils mangent du gâteau. 2/ Nous adorons la musique. 3/ Vous dansez très bien. 4/ Elles jouent aux cartes. 5/ Nous cherchons les toilettes.

Exercise 7.4

1/ Elle finit ses devoirs avant de jouer. 2/ Nous réfléchissons à une solution. 3/ Je rougis quand je le vois. 4/ Vous choisissez quelle option ? 5/ Ils applaudissent quand le spectacle est fini.

Exercise 7.5

1/ Je choisis de partir en vacances. 2/ Elle réussit à finir l'examen à temps. 3/ Il grandit vite. 4/ Tu réfléchis trop. 5/ Il n'obéit pas aux ordres.

Exercise 7.6

1/ Nous attendons le résultat depuis ce matin. 2/ Je prends quelle route pour aller au supermarché ? 3/ Ils vendent de beaux vêtements. 4/ Elle répond au téléphone. 5/ Vous descendez ici ?

Exercise 7.7

1/ Nous attendons depuis longtemps. 2/ Je rends visite à ma grand-mère.
3/ Ils entendent un bruit étrange venant de dehors. 4/ Réponds aux questions.
5/ Nous perdons toujours nos clés.

Exercise 7.8

1/ Il parle bien l'anglais. 2/ Elles répondent à toutes les questions. 3/ Nous choisissons de dormir à l'hôtel ce soir. 4/ J'attends le métro. 5/ Vous marchez assez vite.

DAY 8
THE QUICK WAY TO EXPRESS PAST, PRESENT, AND FUTURE

...or how shortcuts work.

Fancy a quick little jaunt on the express train? I know you do. So, what if I told you that you could actually skip the process of learning verb tenses and instantly learn to talk in French about:

- **recent past**

- **near future**

- **ongoing actions**

Sounds awesome? Certainly is. All this will happen with the use of the **indicative form of the verb**, which is its *basic form*. The best part is, you no longer need to conjugate the verb for the action you're referring to.

1. Expressing recent past using the verb "venir"

"Venir" is an irregular verb which means *"to come"*. When used this way, it can be loosely translated to the English term *"just"*. Such as, *"I just ate"*.

- This is the format to follow: The conjugated present form of **venir + de + the infinitive form of the action that recently happened**.

Use this table for the present forms of venir.

Track 24

Pronoun	Venir form in present tense	Example
Je	viens	**Je viens de manger.** *(I just ate.)*
Tu	viens	**Tu viens de manger.** *(You just ate.)*
Il	vient	**Il vient de manger.** *(He just ate.)*
Nous	venons	**Nous venons de manger.** *(We just ate.)*
Vous	venez	**Vous venez de manger.** *(You just ate.)*
Ils	viennent	**Ils viennent de manger.** *(They just ate.)*

Exercise 8.1 - Complete these sentences to express recent past using the verb "venir":

1. Je _____ (manger) une soupe. *(I just ate a soup.)*

2. Il _____ (sortir). *(He just got out.)*

3. Elle _____ (finir) ses devoirs. *(She just finished her homework.)*

4. Nous _____ (monter) dans le train. *(We just got on the train.)*

5. Ils _____ (partir) pour se reposer. *(They just left to rest.)*

Exercise 8.2 - Transform these sentences to express recent past using the verb "venir":

1. Je parle à mon patron. *(I talk to my boss.)*

   _____

2. Elle prend une douche. *(She takes a shower.)*

   _____

3. Ils finissent leur réunion. *(They finish their meeting.)*

   _____

4. Nous terminons l'examen final. *(We're finishing the final exam.)*

   _____

5. Le professeur explique la nouvelle leçon. *(The teacher explains the new lesson.)*

   _____

2. Expressing the near future using the verb "aller" (futur proche)

Another commonly used irregular French verb is the word **"aller"**. While it literally means *"to go"*, it is also used as a casual way of expressing the near-future tense. Its English counterpart would be saying *"going to"*, such as *"I'm going to sleep in a while."*

- This is the format to follow: The conjugated present form of **aller + the infinitive form of the action that is about to happen**.

Use this table for the present forms of aller, as well as some examples.

Track 25

Pronoun	Aller form in present tense	Example
Je	vais	**Je vais partir.** *(I am going to leave.)*
Tu	vas	**Tu vas partir.** *(You are going to leave.)*
Il	va	**Il va partir.** *(He is going to leave.)*
Nous	allons	**Nous allons partir.** *(We are going to leave.)*
Vous	allez	**Vous allez partir.** *(You are going to leave.)*
Ils	vont	**Ils vont partir.** *(They are going to leave.)*

Exercise 8.3 - Complete these sentences to express the near future using the verb "aller":

1. Je _____ (faire) du ski. *(I am going to ski.)*

2. Nous _____ (jouer) au football. *(We're going to play football.)*

3. Il _____ (essayer) d'écrire un livre. *(He's going to try to write a book.)*

4. Elle _____ (raconter) une histoire aux enfants. *(She's going to read a story to the kids.)*

5. Vous _____ (finir) votre travail un peu tard aujourd'hui. *(You're going to finish your work a bit late today.)*

Exercise 8.4 - Transform these sentences to express the near future using the verb "aller":

1. Je visite la France. *(I visit France.)*

   _____

2. Je me promène dans le parc. *(I walk in the park.)*

   _____

3. Il pleut. *(It's raining.)*

   _____

4. Je prends le train pour aller à Paris. *(I take the train to go to Paris.)*

   _____

5. Ils participent au tournoi de golf. *(They participate in the gold tournament.)*

   _____

3. Expressing ongoing action using the expression "être en train de"

Unlike English, the French language does not have a direct counterpart of the present progressive verb form. The simple present tense is used to mean both simple present and present progressive. But when you fancy being more precise, you can always use the French expression **"être en train de"** which literally means to be "_____-ing" or to be in the middle of doing something.

- This is the format to follow: The conjugated present form of **être** + **en train de** + **the infinitive form of the action that is about to happen.**

Here are the conjugated forms of the irregular verb **"être"** and some examples of how it works.

Track 26

Pronoun	"être" form in present tense	Examples
Je	suis	**Je suis en train de parler.** *I am speaking (right now).*
Tu	es	**Tu es en train de parler.** *You are speaking (right now).*
Il	est	**Il est en train de parler.** *He is speaking (right now).*
Nous	sommes	**Nous sommes en train de parler.** *We are speaking (right now).*
Vous	êtes	**Vous êtes en train de parler.** *You are speaking (right now).*
Ils	sont	**Ils sont en train de parler.** *They are speaking (right now).*

Exercise 8.5 - Complete these sentences to express an ongoing action using the expression "être en train de":

1. Je _____ (boire) du chocolat chaud. *(I am drinking hot chocolate.)*

2. Elle _____ (appeler) sa mère au téléphone. *(She's calling her mother on the phone.)*

3. Nous _____ (faire) le ménage. *(We are doing the household chores.)*

4. Ils _____ (regarder) un film. *(They're watching a movie.)*

5. Vous _____ (perdre) votre temps. *(You are wasting your time.)*

Exercise 8.6 - Transform these sentences to express an ongoing action using the expression "être en train de":

1. Je regarde un film. *(I watch a movie.)*

   _____

2. Je chante sous la douche. *(I sing in the shower.)*

   _____

3. Tu fais de ton mieux. *(You do your best.)*

   _____

4. Il fait de la musique dans sa chambre. *(He makes music in his room.)*

   _____

5. Nous faisons du shopping. *(We're doing shopping.)*

   _____

LET'S PRACTICE SOME MORE!

Exercise 8.7 - Find the right tense:

1. Il _____ arriver au marché. *(He's just arrived at the market.)*

2. Ils _____ se marier en avril. *(They're going to get married in April.)*

3. Jack _____ être diplômé. *(Jack just graduated.)*

4. Je _____ étudier la chimie. *(I am studying chemistry.)*

5. Je _____ rencontrer mon ami. *(I am going to meet my friend.)*

> ***Fun fact:*** French was the official language of England for over 300 years.

Exercise 8.8 - Conjugate the verbs "venir", "aller" and "être" in simple present :

	Venir	Aller	être
Je			
Tu			
Il/Elle			
Nous			
Vous			
Ils/Elles			

ANSWERS:

Exercise 8.1

1/ Je viens de manger une soupe. 2/ Il vient de sortir. 3/ Elle vient de finir ses devoirs. 4/ Nous venons de monter dans le train. 5/ Ils viennent de partir pour se reposer.

Exercise 8.2

1/ Je viens de parler à mon patron. 2/ Elle vient de prendre une douche. 3/ Ils viennent de finir leur reunion. 4/ Nous venons de terminer l'examen final. 5/ Le professeur vient d'expliquer la nouvelle leçon.

Exercise 8.3

1/ Je vais faire du ski. 2/ Nous allons jouer au football. 3/ Il va essayer d'écrire un livre. 4/ Elle va raconter une histoire aux enfants. 5. Vous allez finir votre travail un peu tard aujourd'hui.

Exercise 8.4

1/ Je vais visiter la France. 2/ Je vais me promener dans le parc. 3/ Il va pleuvoir. 4/ Je vais prendre le train pour aller à Paris. 5/ Ils vont participer au tournoi de golf.

Exercise 8.5

1/ Je suis en train de boire du chocolat chaud. 2/ Elle est en train d'appeler sa mère au téléphone. 3/ Nous sommes en train de faire le ménage. 4/ Ils sont en train de regarder un film. 5/ Vous êtes en train de perdre votre temps.

Exercise 8.6

1/ Je suis en train de regarder un film. 2/ Je suis en train de chanter sous la douche. 3/ Tu es en train de faire de ton mieux. 4/ Il est en train de faire de la musique dans sa chambre. 5/ Nous sommes en train de faire du shopping.

Exercise 8.7

Track 27

1/ Il vient d'arriver au marché. 2/ Ils vont se marier en avril. 3/ Jack vient d'être diplômé. 4/ Je suis en train d'étudier la chimie. 5/ Je vais rencontrer mon ami.

Exercise 8.8

	Venir	**Aller**	**être**
Je	viens	vais	suis
Tu	viens	vas	es
Il/Elle	vient	va	est
Nous	venons	allons	sommes
Vous	venez	allez	êtes
Ils/Elles	viennent	vont	sont

DAY 9
"EN" AND "Y"

... or little words that make a huge difference.

Say hello to your new adverbial pronoun friends **"en"** and **"y"**: they're two of a kind and are very important in daily conversing. **"En"** and **"y"** have different uses, and how they are used has different translations in English.

Here are some basic rules to remember about these two.

- **EN**
  - **"En"** is used to replace verbs and phrases which use **"de"**. This is to avoid repeating the same words.
  - It can mean *"some"* or *"any"* when it is not followed by a noun.
    For example:
    - **Avez-vous des chiens ?** *(Do you have any dogs?)*
    - **Oui, nous <u>en</u> avons.** *(Yes, we have some.)*
  - It can also mean *"of it"* or *"of them"*.
    For example:
    - **Ont-ils des chiens ?** *(Do they have any dogs?)*
    - **Oui, ils <u>en</u> ont deux.** *(Yes, they have two of them.)*
  - Another usage is in order to say *"about it"* or *"about them"*.
    For example:
    - **Que penses-tu de mon plan ? Qu'en penses-tu ?**

      (What do you think about my plan? What do you think about it?)

- **Y**
  - **"Y"** is used to replace words and phrases beginning with **"à"**, **"chez"**, or **"dans"** to avoid repetition.
  - It can mean *"there"* when replacing **"dans"** (*in*) or **"sur"** (*on*).
    For example:
    - **Il <u>y</u> passe tout l'été.** *(He spends the whole summer there.)*
  - It can also be used to mean *"to it"* or *"to them"*.

For example:

- o **J'y réponds.** *(I'm responding to it.)*

Word order for "en" and "y"

- In most cases, **en** and **y** come before the verb.
- When used in commands or instructions, **en** and **y** come AFTER the verb and are connected with a hyphen.

  - o Examples: **restez-y** *(stay there)* / **prenez-en** *(take some)*

- **En** and **y** come after direct or indirect object pronouns.

  - o Example: **Elle m'en a parlé.** *(She spoke to me about it.)*

LET'S PRACTICE!

Exercise 9.1 - Answer with "en" or "y":

1. Q: Est-ce que vous prenez du vin avec votre plat ? *(Do you wish to take some wine with your dish?)*

   A: Oui, _____

   B: Non, _____

2. Tu as de l'argent ? *(Do you have some money?)*

   A: Oui, _____

   B: Non, _____

Replace with "y" or "en":

3. Ils sortent du cinéma à 10h. *(They come out of the movie theater at 10pm.)*

   _____

4. Ils vont à la maison. *(They are going to their house.)*

   _____

5. Ils viennent de la bibliothèque. *(They are coming from the library.)*

   _____

6. Les échecs ? Je ne sais pas _ jouer. *(Chess? I don't know how to play.)*

   _____

> ***Fun fact:*** Non-French celebrities who speak French include Jodie Foster, Johnny Depp, Diane Kruger, Elton John, Ewan Mcgregor, Halle Berry, Jackie O, Madonna, Mick Jagger, and John Travolta.

Exercise 9.2 - Choose the correct answer:

1. Demain, je vais chez le dentiste. J'_____ vais tous les ans. *(Tomorrow, I'm going to the dentist. I go there every year.)*

   a. en   b. y

2. Tu peux _____ aller en train. *(You can go there by train.)*

   a. en   b. y

3. Je m'_____ sers pour travailler. *(I use it for work.)*

   a. en   b. y

4. Nous _____ sommes fiers. *(We are proud of it.)*

   a. en   b. y

5. J'_____ ai pensé. *(I thought about it.)*

   a. en   b. y

Exercise 9.3 - Complete these sentences with "en" and "y":

1. "Veux-tu du café ?" "Non, je n'_____ veux pas, merci." *("Do you want some coffee?" "No, thank you.")*

2. Je pars à Paris ce soir. J'_____ vais en train. *(I'm going to Paris tonight. I'm going there by train.)*

3. "As-tu assez d'argent ?" "Oui, j'_____ ai assez." *("Do you have enough money?" "Yes, I do.")*

4. C'est un bon restaurant. Allez_____. *(It's a good restaurant. Go ahead.)*

5. "Vous avez encore des croissants ?" "Oui, nous _____ avons." *("Do you still have some croissant?" "Yes, we do.")*

Exercise 9.4 - Replace the underlined words with "en" and "y":

1. Ils vont <u>à la maison.</u> *(They go to the house.)*

   _____

2. Je vais manger <u>du gâteau.</u> *(I'm going to eat some cake.)*

   _____

3. Je bois <u>du vin</u> très souvent. *(I drink wine very often.)*

   _____

4. Je crois <u>à cette histoire</u>. *(I believe this story.)*

   _____

5. Il veut aller <u>à Nice</u>. *(He wants to go to Nice.)*

   _____

Exercise 9.5 - Answer these questions using "en" and "y":

1. Êtes-vous allés à Paris ? *(Did you go to Paris?)*

   _____

2. Veux-tu du gâteau ? *(Would you like some cake?)*

   _____

3. As-tu acheté du pain ? *(Did you buy bread?)*

   _____

4. Avec qui vas-tu au cinéma ? *(With whom do you go to the cinema?)*

   _____

5. Quand vas-tu à l'école ? *(When are you going to school?)*

   _____

ANSWERS:

Exercise 9.1

Track 28

1/ A: Oui, j'en prends. B: Non, je n'en prends pas. 2/ A: Oui, j'en ai. B: Non, je n'en ai pas. 3/ Ils en sortent. 4/ Ils y vont. 5/ Ils en viennent. 6/ Les échecs ? Je ne sais pas y jouer.

Exercise 9.2

1/ y 2/ y 3/ en 4/ en 5/y

Exercise 9.3

1/ en 2/ y 3/ en 4/ y 5/ en

Exercise 9.4

1/ Ils y vont. 2/ Je vais en manger. 3/ J'en bois très souvent. 4/ J'y crois. 5/ Il veut y aller.

Exercise 9.5

Example answers :

1/ Oui, nous y sommes allés. <u>Or</u> Non, nous n'y sommes pas allés. *(Yes, we went there. No, we didn't go.)*

2/ Oui, j'en veux. <u>Or</u> Non, je n'en veux pas. *(Yes, I want some. No, I don't want it.)*

3 / Oui, j'en ai acheté. Non, je n'en ai pas acheté. *(Yes, I bought some. Gold No, I didn't buy any.)*

4/ J'y vais avec mes amis. *(I go there with my friends)*

5/ J'y vais dans 30 minutes. *(I'm going there in 30 minutes)*

DAY 10
EXPRESSING CAUSES AND RESULTS

Because... it's important.

Whether you're stating your reasons, making an explanation, or discussing the cause and effect of a certain thing, you need these four words to help you out: **"parce que"**, **"car"**, **"puisque"**, and **"comme"**. They're similar, but not identical, and the important thing is they're quite easy to use.

Here are some tips for you:

- **"Parce que"** means *"because"* in English. Like its counterpart, it is used to explain the reason why something was done or to state the motive and cause.

- It can be used in the beginning of a sentence.

- It is a subordinating conjunction and can join two parts of a sentence together.

   Example: **Je ne suis pas allé <u>parce que</u> j'étais malade.**
   (I did not go because I was sick.)

- **"Car"** also means "because" or *"for"*.

- It is considered very formal and not used as often as **parce que**. In fact, you're likely to find **car** in written or formal French speech only.

- You cannot begin a sentence with the word **car**, unlike **parce que**.

   Example: **Le mariage a été annulé <u>car</u> le marié** était **malade.**
   (The wedding was canceled because the groom was sick.)

- **"Puisque"** can also be translated as *"because"* or *"since"*.

- It can be used at the start of the sentence.

- It is used when stating very obvious reasons.

   Example: **<u>Puisque</u> tu es malade, tu peux partir.**
   (Since you are sick, you can leave.)

- The fourth one is **"comme"**, which also means *"since"* or *"as"*.

- It is mostly found in the beginning of a sentence.

- You use it when you want to emphasize the connection between the cause and its effect.

   Example: **Comme il est malade, il peut partir.**
   (As he is sick, he can leave.)

LET'S PRACTICE!

Exercise 10.1 - Choose the right connector between [parce que], [car], [puisque], and [comme]:

1. Elle a dû payer une amende _____elle a conduisait trop vite.

    (She had to pay a fine because she drove too fast.)

2. _____tu es en retard, tu n'iras pas au cinéma.

    (Since you are late, you cannot go to the movie theater.)

3. La rue Vaugirard est fermée _____il y a une manifestation.

    (The Vaugirard Street is closed because there is a protest.)

4. _____il neige, je ne peux pas aller à l'école.

    (As it is snowing, I cannot go to school.)

5. Le match a été annulé _____la météo était mauvaise.

    (The game was cancelled because the weather was bad.)

> ***Fun fact:*** France has the highest number of ski resorts in the world.

Exercise 10.2 - Choose the correct answer:

1. Which one of these words cannot be placed at the beginning of a sentence?

    a. parce que   b. comme   c. puisque   d. car

2. Which one of these is more formal?

    a. car   b. parce que

3. Which one of these is used when stating very obvious reasons?

    a. parce que   b. comme   c. puisque   d. car

4. Which one of these is mostly found at the beginning of a sentence?

    a. parce que   b. comme   c. puisque   d. car

5. Which one of these is used to emphasize the connection between the cause and its effect?

a. parce que   b. puisque   c. car   d. comme

Exercise 10.3 - Use "parce que" to link each group of two sentences:

1. Je suis en train de réviser/ j'ai un examen demain. *(I'm studying./ I have an exam tomorrow.)*

   _____

2. Il va au restaurant/ il a faim. *(He is going to a restaurant./ He's hungry.)*

   _____

3. Elle va au cinéma/ elle veut regarder un film. *(She is going to the cinema./ She wants to see a movie.)*

   _____

4. Nous allons au supermarché/ nous n'avons plus de lait. *(We are going to the supermarket./ We don't have milk anymore.)*

   _____

5. Je vais chez le médecin/ je ne me sens pas très bien. *(I'm going to the doctor./ I don't feel very good.)*

   _____

Exercise 10.4 - Use "car" to link each group of two sentences:

1. Je ne suis pas allé à l'école/ je suis malade. *(I didn't go to school./ I am sick.)*

   _____

2. Je ne prends pas mon petit déjeuner/ je n'ai pas le temps. *(I am not eating breakfast./ I don't have time.)*

   _____

3. Je rends visite à ma grand-mère/ elle est malade. *(I am visiting my grandmother./ she's sick.)*

   _____

4. Elle boit de l'eau/ elle a soif. *(She is drinking water./ She's thirsty.)*

   _____

5. Il achète un ordinateur/ il en a besoin. *(He is buying a computer./ He needs it.)*

_____

Exercise 10.5 - Use "puisque" to link each group of two sentences:

1. Je reste à la maison/ il pleut dehors. *(I am staying at home./ It's raining outside.)*

   _____

2. Je n'utilise pas mon téléphone portable/ il est cassé. *(I don't use my phone./ It's broken.)*

   _____

3. Il ne peut pas acheter une nouvelle voiture/ il n'a pas assez d'argent. *(He can't buy a new car./ He doesn't have enough money.)*

   _____

4. Je prends un taxi/ ma voiture est en panne. *(I am taking a taxi./ my car broke down.)*

Exercise 10.6 - Use "comme" to link each group of two sentences:

1. On a allumé la cheminée/ il fait froid dehors. *(We lit a fire in the fireplace./ It's cold outside.)*

   _____

2. Nous allons à la plage/ il fait chaud. *(We are going to the beach./ The weather is hot.)*

   _____

3. Il se promène dans le parc/ il fait beau. *(He is taking a walk in the park./ The weather is nice.)*

   _____

4. Nous partons en voyage/ c'est les vacances. *(We're going to travel./ It's the holidays.)*

   _____

Exercise 10.7 - Say if the underlined statement is a cause or a result:

1. <u>Je prends le métro</u> car c'est loin. *(I take the metro to go to school because it's far away.)* - _____

2. Je lui achète un cadeau <u>parce que c'est son anniversaire.</u> *(I bought him a gift because it's his birthday.)* - _____

3. <u>Comme c'est dimanche</u>, il va au musée. *(Since it's Sunday, he is going to the museum.)* - _____

Exercise 10.8 - Complete these sentences with [parce que], [car], [puisque], ou [comme]:

1. _____ il était tard, nous avons décidé de rentrer. *(Since it was late, we decided to go home.)*

2. Je veux aller à Paris _____ je veux voir la tour Eiffel. *(I want to go to Paris to see the Eifel Tower.)*

3. Pourquoi ne pas sortir aujourd'hui _____ il fait beau ? *(Why not go out today since the weather is good?)*

Exercise 10.9 - Choose an element from column A and another from column B to create a sentence:

Column A	Column B
1. J'ai fait un gâteau au chocolat	a. car j'aime la couleur rouge.
2. J'ai acheté une robe rouge	b. puisqu'elle est malade.
3. Elle doit se faire soigner	c. parce que j'aime le chocolat.

ANSWERS:

Exercise 10.1

Track 29

1/ Elle a dû payer une amende parce qu'elle a conduisait trop vite. 2/ Puisque tu es en retard, tu n'iras pas au cinema. 3/ La rue Vaugirard est fermée car il y a une manifestation. 4/ Comme il neige, je ne peux pas aller à l'école. 5/ Le match a été annulé car la météo était mauvaise.

Exercise 10.2

1/ car 2/ car 3/ puisque 4/ comme 5/ puisque

Exercise 10.3

1/ Je suis en train de réviser car j'ai un examen demain. 2/ Il va au restaurant parce qu'il a faim. 3/ Elle va au cinéma parce qu'elle veut regarder un film. 4/ Nous allons au supermarché parce que nous n'avons plus de lait. 5/ Je vais chez le médecin parce que je ne me sens pas très bien.

Exercise 10.4

1/ Je ne suis pas allé à l'école car je suis malade. 2/ Je ne prends pas mon petit déjeuner car je n'ai pas le temps. 3/ Je rends visite à ma grand-mère car elle est malade. 4/ Elle boit de l'eau car elle a soif. 5/ Il achète un ordinateur car il en a besoin.

Exercise 10.5

1/ Je reste à la maison puisqu'il pleut dehors. 2/ Je n'utilise pas mon téléphone portable puisqu'il est cassé. 3/ Il ne peut pas acheter une nouvelle voiture puisqu'il n'a pas assez d'argent. 5/ Je prends un taxi puisque ma voiture est en panne.

Exercise 10.6

1/ Comme il fait froid dehors, on a allumé la cheminée. 2/ Comme il fait chaud, nous allons à la plage. 3/ Comme il fait beau, il se promène dans le parc. 4/ Comme c'est les vacances, nous partons en voyage.

Exercise 10.7

1/ a result 2/ a cause 3/ a cause

Exercise 10.8

1/ comme 2/ parce que/car 3/ puisque

Exercise 10.9

1/ c 2/ a 3/ b

...to make sure you never get lost.

Knowing how to ask for the right directions is, of course, a skill that's highly useful to acquire. This is especially if you're planning to take a little jaunt to a French-speaking country anytime soon. If not, don't despair, it's still an important part of learning a new language.

Here is a handy guide about the words and phrases you need to know when asking for and giving directions, and for locating things.

But first, here's how to ask the right things.

Begin with:

Track 30

- **Où se trouve _____?**

This is pronounced as **"oo-stroov"** and means *"Where is the _____?"*. Then insert the name of the places you're trying to locate.

Some common examples:

o **l'aéroport**	(the airport)	o **le musée**	(the museum)
o **l'hôtel _____**	(the _____ hotel)	o **le restaurant**	(the restaurant)
o **la gare**	(the train station)	o **le théâtre**	(the theater)
o **la gare routière**	(the bus station)	o **l'école**	(the school)
o **le centre-ville**	(the town center)	o **le parc**	(the park)
o **la banque**	(the bank)	o **l'épicerie**	(the grocery store)
o **les w.c.**	(the bathroom)	o **l'église**	(the church)
o **l'hôpital**	(the hospital)	o **le bureau de change**	(the money changer)

The answers could be any of the following directions:

Track 31

- **à gauche** *(on/to the left)*
- **tournez à gauche** *(turn left)*
- **à droite** *(on/to the right)*
- **tournez à droite** *(turn right)*
- **tout droit** *(straight)*
- **en face** *(facing / across from)*
- **à côté de** *(next to)*
- **devant** *(in front of)*
- **derrière** *(behind, at the back of)*
- **vers le/la____** *(towards the____)*
- **après le/la____** *(past the____)*
- **en haut** *(uphill)*
- **en bas** *(downhill)*

- **avant le/la____** *(before the____)*
- **repérez le/la__** *(watch for the____)*
- **intersection** *(intersection)*
- **en haut** *(up)*
- **en bas** *(down)*
- **près de** *(near to)*
- **loin de** *(far from)*
- **au nord** *(to the north)*
- **au sud** *(to the south)*
- **à l'est** *(to the east)*
- **à l'ouest** *(to the west)*
- **rue** *(street)*

With this guide, you're unlikely to get lost in any French-speaking country anytime soon. At least, I hope not!

BONUS!!!

How about directions on a smaller scale, such as when you want to know where something is located inside a room? Here are other useful terms for you to take note of.

Track 32

- **Question: où est _____? *(Where is _____?)***

  - **le téléphone portable** *(the cellphone)*
  - **le livre** *(the book)*
  - **la télécommande** *(the remote control)*
  - **mon sac** *(my bag)*
  - **la clé** *(the key)*
  - **mon portefeuille** *(my wallet)*
  - **l'ordinateur** *(the computer)*
  - **l'ordinateur portable** *(the laptop computer)*

Here are the possible answers:

  - **sur** *(on top of)*
  - **sous** *(under)*
  - **devant** *(in front of)*
  - **derrière** *(behind)*
  - **à côté de** *(beside/next to)*
  - **entre** *(between)*

LET'S PRACTICE!

Exercise 11.1 - Choose the right answer:

1. près de

   a. near to   b. next to   c. straight ahead   d. far from

2. Allez tout droit.

   a. Go all the way right.   b. Go all the way.

   c. Go straight.   d. Go very far.

3. C'est à gauche.

   a. It's on the right.   b. It's straight ahead.

   c. It's on the left.   d. It's far away.

4. Où est la bibliothèque ?

   a. Is there a library?   b. What time does the library?

   c. Where is the library?   d. Is the library?

5. The bank is not next to the movie theater.

   a. Le bureau de change n'est pas à côté du cinéma.

   b. La banque est à côté du cinéma.

   c. La banque n'est pas à côté du cinéma.

   d. La banque n'est pas à côté de l'école.

> **Fun fact:** French women have the highest life expectancy of any demographic group in the European Union.

Exercise 11.2 - Choose the correct translation:

1. La banque est en face du parc.

   a. The bank is across from the park.

   b. The bank is near the park.

   c. The bank is far from the park.

2. Tournez à droite. Vous trouverez l'hôtel.

    a. Turn left. You'll find the hotel.

    b. Turn right. You'll find the hotel.

    c. Turn right. The hotel is near.

3. Continuez tout droit.

    a. Go straight.

    b. Continue all right.

    c. Turn right.

Exercise 11.3 - Translate these sentences from French to English:

1. La gare est à côté du parc.

    _____

2. L'épicerie est en face de l'école.

    _____

3. Continuez tout droit. Puis, tournez à gauche à la prochaine intersection. (Puis = then, prochaine = next)

    _____

Exercise 11.4 - Choose the correct translation:

1. The book is under the keys.

    a. Les clés sont sous le livre.

    b. Le livre est sous les clés.

    c. Le livre est sur les clés.

2. Où est la télécommande?

    a. Where is the remote control?

    b. Where is the television?

    c. The remote control is in front of the television.

3. Mon portefeuille est sur mon sac.

    a. My wallet is in my bag.

    b. My wallet is on my bag.

    c. My wallet is under my bag.

Exercise 11.5 - Complete the sentences with these words : [à gauche], [à droite], [tout droit], [en face de] and [loin de] (each word is used at most once):

1. Le théâtre est près de la banque. Il est juste _____ elle. *(The theater is near the bank. He's just _____ her.)*

2. Tournez _____ ! *(Turn _____!)*

3. Continuez _____. *(Continue _____.)*

4. L'hôpital est _____ ici. *(The hospital is _____ here.)*

Exercise 11.6 - Translate these sentences from English to French:

1. The cellphone is on the book.

   _____

2. The book is in front of the bag.

   _____

3. The keys are next to the computer.

   _____

Exercise 11.7 - Complete the sentences with these words: [à côté], [entre], and [devant]:

1. Mon téléphone portable est _____ mon ordinateur et mon sac. *(My cell phone is _____ my computer and my bag.)*

2. Tes clés sont _____ de ton sac. *(Your keys are _____ from your bag.)*

3. La télécommande est _____ la télé. (télé = télévision) *(The remote control is _____ the TV.)*

ANSWERS:

Exercise 11.1

1/ near to 2/ Go straight. 3/ It's on the left. 4/ Where is the library? 5/ La banque n'est pas à côté du cinéma.

Exercise 11.2

1/ The bank is across from the park. 2/ Turn right. You'll find the hotel. 3/ Go straight.

Exercise 11.3

1/ The train station is next to the park. 2/ The grocery store is across from the school. 3/ Go straight. Then, turn left at the next intersection.

Exercise 11.4

1/ Le livre est sous les clés. 2/ Where is the remote control? 3/ My wallet is on my bag.

Exercise 11.5

1/ en face d' 2/ à gauche or à droite 3/ tout droit 4/ loin d'

Exercise 11.6

1/ Le téléphone portable est sur le livre. 2/ Le livre est devant le sac. 3/ Les clés sont près de l'ordinateur.

Exercise 11.7

1/ entre 2/ à côté 3/ devant

DAY 12
USING *AVOIR* IN THE PERFECT TENSE

Before we jump into anything else, let's start by talking about the **French perfect tense**. It is also known as **"passé composé"** or **"compound past"** because it consists of two parts: an **auxiliary verb** and the **past participle**.

We use the perfect tense to talk about an action that was fully completed in the past. In English, it can be identified by the word *"have"* that accompanies it. For example: *"I have eaten"*. The verb consists of two parts too: *"have"* and *"eaten"*. It basically works the same way in French.

The auxiliary verbs that accompany the perfect tense could either be **"avoir"** (*to have*) or **"être"** (*to be*). For this lesson, we will focus on **"avoir"**.

Here are the most important things you should know when using avoir in the perfect tense.

- **Avoir** is used more often than **être**. (See the next lesson for when to use **être**.)

- This is the format to use when forming the perfect tense with **avoir**:

The present tense of the verb **avoir** + **the past participle**.

Choose from the following present tense forms of avoir:

1st person singular	**j'ai**	*(I have)*
2nd person singular	**tu as**	*(you have)*
3rd person singular	**il/elle a**	*(he has or she has)*
1st person plural	**nous avons**	*(we have)*
2nd person plural	**vous avez**	*(you have)*
3rd person plural	**ils/elles ont**	*(they have)*

Now, to form the past participle, here are the rules.

- First, start with the infinitive of the verb, and then proceed to the following changes in the ending.

- If the infinitive ends with an **-er**, replace the **-er** with **-é**.

- Examples: **donner** becomes **donné**; **tomber** becomes **tombé**

- If the infinitive ends with an **-ir**, remove the **r** at the end

- Examples: **finir** becomes **fini**; **partir** becomes **parti**

- If the infinitive ends with a **-re**, replace the -re with **-u**.

- Examples: **attendre** becomes **attendu**, **descendre** becomes **descendu**.

Using the formula above, let us take a look at a few examples:

Track 33

Pronoun + avoir	+ past participle	= perfect tense formed	meaning in English
J'ai	donné	J'ai donné	*(I have given)*
Tu as	donné	Tu as donné	*(You have given)*

LET'S PRACTICE!

Exercise 12.1 - Give the passé composé of the verb indicated in parentheses:

1. Tu _____ du jus d'orange ? (boire) *(Do you ____ orange juice?) (to drink)*

2. J' _____ de nouveaux poèmes. (écrire) *(I ____ new poems.) (to write)*

3. Nous _____ le match de foot. (regarder) *(We _____ the soccer game.) (watch)*

4. Jean et David _____ leurs parents hier soir. (rencontrer) *(Jean and David ____ their parents last night.) (meet)*

5. Il _____ beaucoup de gâteaux pour la fête. (préparer) *(He ____ a lot of cakes for the party.) (to prepare)*

6. Luc_____ visite à Lisa. (rendre) *(Luke____ visit Lisa.) (return)*

7. Cédric et Julie _____ du shopping hier. (faire) *(Cédric and Julie ____ from shopping yesterday.) (make)*

8. Est-ce que vous _____ les moteurs ? (voir) *(Do you ____ the engines?) (see)*

> ***Fun fact:*** Wearing a white wedding dress is a French tradition which began in 1499.

Exercise 12.2 - Conjugate the verb "avoir" in the present tense:

Je _____

Tu _____

Il/Elle _____

Nous _____

Vous _____

Ils/Elles _____

Exercise 12.3 - Conjugate the verb "donner" (to give), "finir" (to finish) and "boire" (to drink) in the perfect tense:

	Donner	Finir	Boire
Je			
Tu			
Il/elle			
Nous			
Vous			
Ils/elles			

Exercise 12.4 - Conjugate the verbs between brackets in the perfect tense:

1. Nous (boire) _____ quelques verres ensemble. *(We drank some glasses together.)*

2. Je (écrire) _____ une lettre à ma petite amie. *(I wrote a letter to my girlfriend.)*

3. Vous (regarder) _____ le match de foot d'hier ? *(Did you watch yesterday's football game?)*

4. Je (rencontrer) _____ ma meilleure amie quand j'étais enfant. *(I met my best friend when I was a kid.)*

5. Ils (préparer) _____ un gâteau d'anniversaire pour leur sœur. *(They made a birthday cake for their sister.)*

Exercise 12.5 - Change the pronouns from plural to singular and rewrite the sentences:

1. Nous avons rendu visite à notre tante. *(We visited our aunt.)*

   _____

2. Bravo ! Vous avez fait des progrès ! *(Congratulations! You have made progress!)*

   _____

3. Ils ont vu le nouveau film de Superman. *(They saw the new Superman movie.)*

   _____

4. Qu'est-ce que vous avez mangé hier soir ? *(What did you eat yesterday?)*

———————————————————————

5. Elles ont monté les escaliers. *(They went up the stairs.)*

———————————————————————

Exercise 12.6 - These sentences are given in the simple present tense. Change them into the perfect tense:

1. Je perds mon temps. *(I'm wasting my time.)*

———————————————————————

2. Il lit un livre. *(He reads a book.)*

———————————————————————

3. Ils réalisent leurs rêves. *(They realize their dreams.)*

———————————————————————

4. Est-ce que vous y croyez ? *(Do you believe it?)*

———————————————————————

5. Qu'est-ce que tu prépares ? *(What are you preparing?)*

———————————————————————

ANSWERS:

Exercise 12.1
Track 34

1/ Tu as bu du jus d'orange ? 2/ J'ai écrit de nouveaux poèmes. 3/ Nous avons regardé le match de foot. 4/ Jean et David ont rencontré leurs parents hier soir. 5/ Il a préparé beaucoup de gâteaux pour la fête. 6/ Luc a rendu visite à Lisa. 7/ Cédric et Julie ont fait du shopping hier. 8/ Est-ce que vous avez vu les moteurs ?

Exercise 12.2:

J'ai / Tu as / Il/Elle a / Nous avons / Vous avez / Ils/Elles ont

Exercise 12.3

	Donner	**Finir**	**Boire**
Je	ai donné	ai fini	ai bu
Tu	as donné	as fini	as bu
Il/elle	a donné	a fini	a bu
Nous	avons donné	avons fini	avons bu
Vous	avez donné	avez fini	avez bu
Ils/elles	ont donné	ont fini	ont bu

Exercise 12.4

1/ Nous avons bu quelques verres ensemble. 2/ J'ai écrit une lettre à ma petite amie. 3/ Vous avez regardé le match de foot d'hier ? 4/ J'ai rencontré ma meilleure amie quand j'étais enfant. 5/ Ils ont préparé un gâteau d'anniversaire pour leur sœur.

Exercise 12.5

1/ J'ai rendu visite à ma tante. 2/ Bravo ! Tu as fait des progrès ! 3/ Il a vu le nouveau film de Superman. 4/ Qu'est-ce que tu as mangé hier soir ? 5/ Elle a monté les escaliers.

Exercise 12.6

1/ J'ai perdu mon temps. 2/ Il a lu un livre. 3/ Ils ont réalisé leurs rêves. 4/ Est-ce que vous y avez cru ? 5/ Qu'est-ce que tu as préparé ?

DAY 13
USING "ÊTRE" IN THE PERFECT TENSE

While the previous lesson explored using **"avoir"** in forming the perfect tense, for this one we will focus on the second auxiliary verb in the perfect tense: **"être"**.

Here are the important things to remember:

- The format is quite similar to the previous one.

   The present tense of the verb **être + the past participle**.

- These are the present tense forms of **être** together with the corresponding pronouns.
   - **je suis**
   - **tu es**
   - **il est**
   - **nous sommes**
   - **vous êtes**
   - **ils sont**

As mentioned in lesson 12, **être** is not used as often as **avoir** in the perfect tense. Given this, the question is: when do you use it?

There are two groups of verbs that make use of **être**.

1. Reflexive verbs

When we say reflexive verbs, we mean the French verbs that appear with the pronoun se or the shortened form **s'** before it. These action words are used when the subject is the same person as the object. To put it simply, it means *"to_____ oneself"*.

Take, for example, the verb **"habiller"** which means *"to get dressed"*.

Track 35

Pronoun + être	+ Past participle	Perfect tense formed	Meaning in English
je me suis	**habillé**	**je me suis habillé**	*(I got dressed)*
tu t'es	**habillé**	**tu t'es habillé**	*(you got dressed)*
il s'est	**habillé**	**il s'est habillé**	*(he got dressed)*

elle s'est	**habillée**	**elle s'est habillée**	(she got dressed)
nous nous sommes	**habillés**	**nous nous sommes habillés**	(we got dressed)
vous vous êtes	**habillés**	**vous vous êtes habillés**	(you got dressed)
ils se sont	**habillés**	**ils se sont habillés**	(they got dressed)
elles se sont	**habillées**	**elles se sont habillées**	(they got dressed)

2. A selected group of verbs that mostly refer to or involve bodily movement or some kind of physical activity.
Track 36

Some common examples:

- **aller** *(to go)*
- **venir** *(to come)*
- **arriver** *(to arrive)*
- **partir** *(to leave/go)*
- **mourir** *(to die)*
- **naître** *(to be born)*
- **devenir** *(to become)*
- **rester** *(to stay)*

- **descendre** *(to go down)*
- **monter** *(to go up)*
- **entrer** *(to go in/ come in)*
- **sortir** *(to go out)*
- **tomber** *(to fall)*
- **retourner** *(to go back/ return)*
- **rentrer** *(to come back/ come home)*

Even more rules:

- To form the past participle when using **être**, the past participle has to agree with the subject of the verb.

Therefore, their endings change to accommodate the masculine and feminine, as well as the singular and plural forms.

Here are the two steps to form the past participle for verbs that use être.

Step 1: Change the infinitive

- If the infinitive ends with an **-er**, replace the -er with **-é**.
- If the infinitive ends with an **-ir**, remove the **r** at the end.

- If the infinitive ends with a -**re**, replace the -**re** with -**u**.

Step 2: Add the correct endings

- To form a masculine plural past participle, you add -**s**.
- To form a feminine singular past participle, you add -**e**.
- To form a feminine plural past participle, you add -**es**.

Examples:

	Masculine endings	Examples	Feminine Endings	Examples
Singular	-	tombé parti descendu	-e	tombée partie descendue
Plural	-s	tombés partis descendus	-es	tombées parties descendues

Some examples using the format.

Track 37

Je suis tombé. (masculine)	(I have fallen.)	**Je suis tombée.** (feminine)
Tu es tombé. (masculine)	(You have fallen.)	**Tu es tombée.** (feminine)
Il est tombé.	(He/it has fallen. She/it has fallen (for elle...))	**Elle est tombée.**
Nous sommes tombés. (masculine)	(We have fallen.)	**Nous sommes tombées.** (feminine)
Vous êtes tombés. (masculine)	(You have fallen.)	**Vous êtes tombées.** (feminine)
Ils sont tombés.	(They have fallen.)	**Elles sont tombées.** (feminine)

LET'S PRACTICE!

Exercise 13.1 - Give the passé composé of the verb indicated in brackets:

1. Cyril _____ en France il y a un an. (aller) *(Cyril ____ in France a year ago.) (go)*

2. Pierre _____ en retard, comme toujours. (arriver) *(Pierre ____ late, as always.) (arrive)*

3. Hier, Julie _____ durant le cours de yoga. (tomber) *(Yesterday, Julie ____ during the yoga class.) (fall)*

4. Je _____ à la maison hier soir. (rester) *(I ____ at home last night.) (stay)*

5. Vous _____ très tard après la fête. (rentrer) *(You ____ very late after the party.) (enter)*

6. Dominique et Sophie_____ ensemble. (venir) *(Dominique and Sophie____ together.) (come)*

7. Marie_____ en mai. (naître) *(Marie____ in May.) (to be born)*

8. Pourquoi est-ce que vous _____ avec Bette ? (partir) *(Why are you ____ with Bette?) (go)*

> ***Fun fact:*** There are more than 1,000 different kinds of cheese made in France.

Exercise 13.2 - Conjugate the verb "être" in the present tense:

Je _____

Tu _____

Il/Elle _____

Nous _____

Vous _____

Ils/Elles _____

Exercise 13.3: Conjugate the verb "s'habiller" (to get dressed), "se laver" (to wash oneself) and "se coucher" (to go to bed) in the perfect tense. What are these verbs called?

	S'habiller	Se laver	Se coucher
Je			
Tu			
Il			
Elle			
Nous			
Vous			
Ils			
Elles			

Exercise 13.4 - Conjugate the verbs in brackets in the perfect tense:

1. Il (venir) _____ tout seul. *(He came alone.)*

2. Nous (sortir) _____ ensemble l'année dernière. *(We went out together last year.)*

3. Je (reste) _____ à la maison hier. *(I stayed home yesterday.)*

4. Elle (naître) _____ le 10 décembre. *(She was born on December 10th.)*

5. Vous (aller) _____ à l'école ? *(Did you go to school?)*

Exercise 13.5 - Change the pronouns from plural to singular and rewrite the sentences:

1. Ils sont devenus vieux. *(They became old.)*

   _____

2. Elles sont parties hier. *(They left yesterday.)*

   _____

3. Vous êtes arrivés quand ? *(When did you arrive?)*

   _____

4. Nos voitures sont tombées en panne. *(Our cars broke down.)*

_____

5. Nous sommes tombés de la falaise. *(We fell off the cliff.)*

_____

Exercise 13.6 - These sentences are given in the simple present tense. Change them into the perfect tense:

1. Je vais à la maison. *(I go to the house.)*

_____

2. Il entre dans la salle. *(He enters the room.)*

_____

3. Je sors acheter du pain. *(I go out to buy bread.)*

_____

4. Elles rentrent tard. *(I come home late.)*

_____

5. Tu pars quand ? *(When do you leave?)*

_____

ANSWERS:

Exercise 13.1
Track 38

1/ Cyril est allé en France il y a un an. 2/ Pierre est arrivé en retard, comme toujours. 3/ Hier, Julie est tombée durant le cours de yoga. 4/ Je suis resté à la maison hier soir. 5/ Vous êtes rentrés très tard après la fête. 6/ Dominique et Sophie sont venues ensemble. 7/ Marie est née en mai. 8/ Pourquoi est-ce que vous êtes partis avec Bette ?

Exercise 13.2

Je suis
Tu es
Il/Elle est
Nous sommes
Vous êtes
Ils/Elles sont

Exercise 13.3

	S'habiller	Se laver	Se coucher
Je	me suis habillé	me suis lavé	me suis couché
Tu	t'es habillé	t'es lavé	t'es couché
Il	s'est habillé	s'est lavé	s'est couché
Elle	s'est habillée	s'est lavée	s'est couchée
Nous	nous sommes habillés	nous sommes lavés	nous sommes couchés
Vous	vous êtes habillés	vous êtes lavés	vous êtes couchés
Ils	se sont habillés	se sont lavés	se sont couchés
Elles	se sont habillées	se sont lavées	se sont couchées

These are called reflexive verbs.

Exercise 13.4

1/ Il est venu tout seul. 2/ Nous sommes sorti(e)s ensemble l'année dernière. 3/Je suis resté(e) à la maison hier. 4/ Elle est née le 10 décembre. 5/ Vous êtes allé(e)s à l'école ?

Exercise 13.5

1/ Il est devenu vieux. 2/ Elle est partie hier. 3/ Tu es arrivé(e) quand ? 4/ Ma voiture est tombée en panne. 5/ Je suis tombé(e) de la falaise.

Exercise 13.6

1/ Je suis allé(e) à la maison. 2/ Il est entré dans la salle. 3/ Je suis sorti(e) acheter du pain. 4/ Elles sont rentrées tard. 5/ Tu es parti(e) quand ?

DAY 14
THE IMPERFECT TENSE

...or when past events aren't directly specified

We call it **"imparfait"**. It is the verb tense used to talk about past events, especially in descriptions. Unlike the perfect tense, which is used for events that were fully completed, the imperfect tense does not imply a beginning or ending of an action.

In English, you're probably unaware it even exists. Unlike other languages, English doesn't make use of the imperfect tense, but rather uses the past progressive to denote continuous action and the simple past to express a previous state.

We use the imperfect tense:

- To give a physical or emotional description of a past event.

  Example: *It was raining so hard.*

- To talk about a past habitual occurrence or state of being.

  Example: *I used to like her a lot.*

- To indicate an action that was ongoing when something else took place.

  Example: *We were walking our dog when the aliens came.*

In English, we simply say *"was _____"*, *"was _____- ing"* or *"used to_____"*.

Here are some important things to keep in mind when forming the imperfect tense:

- To conjugate a verb into the imperfect, you only need to change the ending of the verb.

- For verbs that end in **-er** and **-re**, use the infinitive, but chop off the **-er** or the **-re** ending.

- Afterwards, add the new ending based on the subject.

- For **-er** and **-re** verbs, the imperfect tense endings are **-ais, -ais, -ait, -ions, -iez, -aient.**

- Using the verb **"donner"** *(to give)* as an example for **-er** verbs, here's what happens when we add the ending:

Track 39

o **Je donnais**	*(I gave, I was giving, I used to give)*
o **Tu donnais**	*(you gave, you were giving, you used to give)*
o **Il/elle/on donnait**	*(he/she/one gave/was giving/used to give)*
o **Nous donnions**	*(we gave, we were giving, we used to give)*
o **Vous donniez**	*(you gave, you were giving, you used to give)*
o **Ils/elles donnaient**	*(they gave, they were giving, they used to give)*

- For -**re** verbs, let's use **"attendre"** *(to wait)*. With the correct endings, here's what becomes of it in the imperfect tense:

Track 40

o J'attendais	*(I waited, I was waiting, I used to wait)*
o Tu attendais	*(you waited, you were waiting, you used to wait)*
o Il attendait	*(he/she/one waited/was waiting/used to wait)*
o Nous attendions	*(we waited, we were waiting, we used to wait)*
o Vous attendiez	*you waited, you were waiting, you used to wait)*
o Ils/elles attendaient	*(they waited, they were waiting, they used to wait)*

- For verbs than end in -**ir** such as **"finir"** *(to finish)*, simply emove the -**ir** and add the appropriate endings.

- For -**ir** verbs, the endings are -**issais, -issais, -issait, -issions, -issiez, -issaient.**

- Using the verb finir as an example, here are the results with the new endings:

Track 41

o Je finissais	*(I finished, I was finishing, I used to finish)*
o Tu finissais	*(you finished, you were finishing, you used to finish)*
o Il/elle/on finissait	*(he/she/one finished/was finishing/used to finish)*
o Nous finissions	*(we finished, we were finishing, we used to finish)*
o Vous finissiez	*(you finished, you were finishing, you used to finish)*
o Ils/elles finissaient	*(they finished, they were finishing, they used to finish)*

LET'S PRACTICE!

Exercise 14.1 - Give the imperfect form of the verb indicated in brackets:

1. Jean et Luc _____ la table quand Lisa a téléphoné. (mettre) *(Jean and Luc ____ the table when Lisa called.) (to put)*

2. Sophie _____ la biologie avant la soirée. (étudier) *(Sophie ____ biology before the party.) (to study)*

3. Je _____ des noisettes quand il a commencé à pleuvoir. (ramasser) *(I ____ nuts when it started to rain.) (to pick up)*

4. J'_____ de la musique classique quand David est arrivé. (écouter) *(I ____ classical music when David arrived.) (listen)*

5. Nous _____ nos exercices quand le cours a commencé. (finir) *(We ____ our exercises when class started.) (finish)*

6. Tu _____ de l'alcool toute la soirée ? (boire) *(Do you ____ alcohol all night?) (to drink)*

7. Vous _____ des rumeurs pendant le cours ? (entendre) *(Do you ____ hear any rumors during class?) (hear)*

8. Julie _____ à son amitié avec Jean quand Sophie est arrivée. (réfléchir) *(Julie ____ to her friendship with Jean when Sophie arrived.) (reflect)*

> ***Fun fact:*** The French national anthem is called la Marseillaise because it was first sung by soldiers from Marseille marching to Paris.

Exercise 14.2 - Conjugate "écouter" (to listen), "réfléchir" (to think), and "mettre" (tu put) in the imperfect tense:

	écouter	réfléchir	mettre
Je			
Tu			
Il/elle			
Nous			
Vous			
Ils/elles			

Exercise 14.3 - Conjugate the verbs in brackets in the imperfect tense:

1. Je (faire) _____ le ménage pendant que mon père cuisinait. (*I was doing the household chores while my dad was cooking.*)

2. Il (attendre) _____ ce résultat avec impatience. (*He was impatiently waiting for the results.*)

3. Tous les jours, ils (courir) _____ dans le parc. (*Every day, they ran in the park.*)

4. Nous (chanter) _____ ensemble. (*We used to sing together.*)

5. Vous (être) _____ amis, n'est-ce pas ? (*You used to be friends, right ?*)

Exercise 14.4 - Change the pronouns from singular to plural then rewrite the sentences:

1. Il était gentil. (*He was kind.*)

   _____

2. Je mangeais souvent dans ce restaurant quand je vivais ici. (*I often ate at this restaurant when I used to live here.*)

   _____

3. Elle apprenait la danse dans cet établissement. (*She was learning dance in this school.*)

   _____

4. Tu étais inconscient. *(You were unconscious.)*

_____

5. Je travaillais très dur pendant qu'il était assis à ne rien faire. *(I was working very hard while he was sitting doing nothing.)*

_____

Exercise 14.5 - Change the pronouns from plural to singular then rewrite the sentences:

1. Nous grimpions à cet arbre quand nous étions enfants. *(We used to climb this tree when we were kids.)*

_____

2. Vous le voyiez souvent, n'est-ce pas ? *(You were always seeing him, weren't you?)*

_____

3. Elles aimaient voyager en train. *(They liked/used to like to travel by train.)*

_____

4. Nous allions quelquefois au cinéma. *(We went/used to go to the cinema sometimes.)*

_____

5. Des arbres entouraient la maison. *(Trees surrounded/used to surround the house.)*

_____

Exercise 14.6 - Conjugate the verbs in brackets in the imperfect tense:

1. Je (faire) _____ du sport tous les jours quand j'avais le temps. *(I used to practice sports every day when I had time.)*

2. Le ciel (être) _____ nuageux. *(The sky was cloudy.)*

3. Nous (passer) _____ notre temps à lire. *(We spent our time reading.)*

4. Elle (prendre) _____ le bus tous les jours. *(She used to take the bus every day.)*

5. Mon grand-père (lire) _____ le journal tous les matins. *(My grandfather used to read the newspaper every morning.)*

ANSWERS:

Exercise 14.1

Track 42

1/ Jean et Luc mettaient la table quand Lisa a téléphoné. 2/ Sophie étudiait la biologie avant la soirée. 3/ Je ramassais des noisettes quand il a commencé à pleuvoir. 4/ J'écoutais de la musique classique quand David est arrivé. 5/ Nous finissions nos exercices quand le cours a commencé. 6/ Tu buvais de l'alcool toute la soirée ? 7/ Vous entendiez des rumeurs pendant le cours ? 8/ Julie réfléchissait à son amitié avec Jean quand Sophie est arrivée.

Exercise 14.2

	écouter	**réfléchir**	**mettre**
Je	écoutais	réfléchissais	mettais
Tu	écoutais	réfléchissais	mettais
Il/elle	écoutait	réfléchissait	mettait
Nous	écoutions	réfléchissions	mettions
Vous	écoutiez	réfléchissiez	mettiez
Ils/elles	écoutaient	réfléchissaient	mettaient

Exercise 14.3

1/ Je faisais le ménage pendant que mon père cuisinait. 2/ Il attendait ce résultat avec impatience. 3/ Tous les jours, ils couraient dans le parc. 4/ Nous chantions ensemble. 5/ Vous étiez amis, n'est-ce pas ?

Exercise 14.4

1/ Ils étaient gentils. 2/ Nous mangions souvent dans ce restaurant quand nous vivions ici. 3/ Elles apprenaient la danse dans cet établissement. 4/ Vous étiez inconscients. 5/ Nous travaillons très dur pendant qu'ils étaient assis à ne rien faire.

Exercise 14.5

1/ Je grimpais à cet arbre quand j'étais enfant. 2/ Tu le voyais souvent, n'est-ce pas? 3/ Elle aimait voyager en train. 4/ J'allais quelquefois au cinéma. 5/ Un arbre entourait la maison.

Exercise 14.6

1/ Je faisais du sport tous les jours quand j'avais le temps. 2/ Le ciel était nuageux. 3/ Nous passions notre temps à lire. 4/ Elle prenait le bus tous les jours. 5/ Mon grand-père lisait le journal tous les matins.

DAY 15
THE IMPERATIVE

Imagine a world where there are no commands or orders being given. Well, yeah, that's right, you can't. Whether you're the one telling people what to do, or you're the one on the receiving end, the world seems to run on commands.

To issue commands or give instructions, we use the imperative form of the verb.

Its other uses are:

- to express a desire (which is basically still a form of issuing a command, only said a lot more nicely).

- to make a request (a very, very polite kind of command).

- to give advice (still a form of command if we come to think of it).

- to recommend something (thus far, still a command cloaked in a helpful kinda coat).

Here is a list of important things to learn about the imperative in French, or the **"imperatif"**.

- There are three forms used for the imperative. Two are commonly used, and these correspond to **"tu"** and **"vous"**. The third form **"nous"** is used sometimes, and it works the same way we say *"let's"* in English.

- Unlike the other verb forms and grammatical moods, the imperative does not use subject pronouns.

- To form the present tense imperative, simply use the present indicative forms for tu, nous, and vous without mentioning these pronouns.

- The conjugation is basically the same as the present tense except that for -**er** verbs, the last -**s** is dropped in the **tu** form.

  Example for verbs ending in -**er: "donner"** becomes **(tu) donne, (nous) donnons**, (vous) donnez.

  o **Donne-moi ça !** *(Give me that!)*

  Example for verbs ending in -**ir: "finir"** becomes **(tu) finis, (nous) finissons, (vous) finissez.**

  o **Finissez vos devoirs.** *(Finish your homework.)*

Example for verbs ending in **-re: "attendre"** becomes **(tu) attends, (nous) attendons, (vous) attendez.**

  o **Attendons le bus.** *(Let's wait for the bus.)*

- There are two kinds of commands where the imperative is used: **affirmative commands** and **negative commands.** An affirmative command would be something like, *"Do this!"* while the negative command is its opposite, *"Don't do that!"*

- In French, the object pronoun which accompanies the imperative changes its position depending on the kind of command being issued.

Track 43

- For affirmative commands, the object pronouns come after the verb. The verb and the pronoun are then linked together with a hyphen.

  Example: **Excusez-moi.** *(Excuse me.)*

- For negative commands, the object pronouns come before the verb. And **ne... pas** is used.

  Example: **Ne leur parlons pas.** *(Don't speak to them.)*

- In cases where both direct and indirect object pronouns are present, the DIRECT OBJECT PRONOUNS always come BEFORE the INDIRECT OBJECT PRONOUNS.

  Example: **Donnez-la-nous !** *(Give it to us!)*

Direct object pronouns	**le, la, les**
Indirect object pronouns	**moi, toi, lui, nous, vous, leur**

LET'S PRACTICE!

Exercise 15.1 - Fill in the blanks with the imperative form of the verb in brackets:

1. _____ Jean ! On étaient si heureux à Lyon ! (se rappeler) (__ *John! We were so happy in Lyon!*) *(to remember)*

2. Lisa, _____ tes légumes ! (finir) *(Lisa, __ your vegetables!) (finish)*

3. _____ de nous disputer ! (arrêter) (__ *to argue!) (Stop)*

4. _____ prétentieux, David ! (ne pas être) (__ *pretentious, David!) (not to be)*

5. _____ rester modestes ! (savoir) (__ *stay modest!) (know)*

6. _____ chez le coiffeur Benjamin ! (aller) (__ *at the hairdresser Benjamin!) (go)*

7. Tu as envie d'aller chez ta copine, Jean ? _____ y ! (aller) *(Do you want to go to your girlfriend's house, Jean? __ y!) (go)*

8. J'achète de la bière ? David : Oui_____en plusieurs bouteilles ! (acheter) *(Am I buying beer? David: Yes __ in several bottles!) (buy)*

> **Fun fact:** The Statue of Liberty was made in France and then gifted to the U.S. on the celebration of the country's centennial year in 1886.

Exercise 15.2 - Conjugate "écouter" (to listen), "réfléchir" (to think) and "mettre" (tu put) in the imperative form:

	écouter	réfléchir	mettre
Tu Nous Vous			

Exercise 15.3 - Conjugate the verbs in brackets in the imperative form:

1. _____ toi les mains avant de manger. (laver) *(Wash your hands before you eat.)*

2. _____ bien ce que je vous dis. (écouter) *(Listen well to what I'm telling you.)*

3. _____ vos ceintures. (attacher) *(Fasten your seatbelts.)*

4. _____ confiance en moi ! (avoir) *(Trust me.)*

5. _____ à gauche à la prochaine intersection, puis continuez tout droit. (tourner) *(Turn left at the next intersection, then continue straight.)*

Exercise 15.4 - Change the pronouns from singular to plural and rewrite the sentences:

1. Dépêche-toi. On va être en retard. *(Hurry up. We're going to be late.)*

   _____

2. Finis ta soupe. *(Finish your soup.)*

   _____

3. Prends le bus. C'est plus rapide. *(Take the bus. It's faster.)*

   _____

4. Sois à l'heure la prochaine fois. *(Be on time next time.)*

   _____

5. Viens avec moi. *(Come with me.)*

   _____

Exercise 15.5 - These sentences are given in the simple present tense form. Change them into the imperative form and make the necessary changes:

1. Tu manges tes légumes. *(You eat his vegetables.)*

   _____

2. Tu me donnes ton numéro. *(You give me her number.)*

   _____

3. Vous éteignez la lumière avant de sortir de la salle. *(You turn off the light before you leave the room.)*

_____

4. Nous partons en vacances cet été. *(We're going on vacation this summer.)*

_____

5. Tu téléphones au directeur. *(You call the director.)*

_____

Exercise 15.6 - Change the pronouns from plural to singular and rewrite the sentences:

1. Prenez soin de vous. *(Take care of yourselves.)*

_____

2. Souhaitez-moi bonne chance. *(Wish me good luck.)*

_____

3. Envoyez-moi un email. *(Send me an email.)*

_____

4. Entendez-vous un bruit ? *(Do you hear a sound?)*

_____

5. Ne vous découragez pas ! *(Don't be discouraged!)*

_____

Exercise 15.7 - Conjugate the verbs in brackets in the imperative form:

1. _____-moi un café, s'il vous plaît. (donner) *(Give me a coffee, please.)*

2. _____ ta chambre tout de suite ! (ranger) *(Clean up your room immediately!)*

3. _____ -moi le sel. (passer) *(Hand me the salt.)*

4. _____ tes devoirs avant de regarder la télé. (faire) *(Do your homework before watching TV.)*

5. N'_____ pas d'apporter vos ordinateurs portables. (oublier) *(Don't forget to bring your laptops.)*

ANSWERS:

Exercise 15.1
Track 44

1/ Rappelle-toi Jean ! On étaient si heureux à Lyon ! (se rappeler) 2/ Lisa, finis tes légumes ! (finir) 3/ Arrêtons de nous disputer ! (arrêter) 4/ Ne sois pas prétentieux, David ! (ne pas être) 5/ Sachons rester modestes ! (savoir) 6/ Va chez le coiffeur Benjamin ! (aller) 7/ Tu as envie d'aller chez ta copine, Jean ? Vas-y ! (aller) 8/ J'achète de la bière ? David : Oui, achètes-en plusieurs bouteilles ! (acheter)

Exercise 15.2

	écouter	**réfléchir**	**mettre**
(Tu)	écoute	réfléchis	mets
(Nous)	écoutons	réfléchissons	mettons
(Vous)	écoutez	réfléchissez	mettez

Exercise 15.3

1/ Lave-toi les mains avant de manger. 2/ Écoutez bien ce que je vous dis. 3/ Attachez vos ceintures. 4/ Aie confiance en moi ! 5/ Tournez à gauche à la prochaine intersection, puis continuez tout droit.

Exercise 15.4

1/ Dépêchez-vous. On va être en retard. 2/ Finissez vos soupes. 3/ Prenez le bus. C'est plus rapide. 4/ Soyez à l'heure la prochaine fois. 5/ Venez avec moi.

Exercise 15.5

1/ Mange tes légumes. 2/ Donne-moi ton numéro. 3/ Éteignez la lumière avant de sortir de la salle. 4/ Partons en vacances cet été. 5/ Téléphone au directeur.

Exercise 15.6

1/ Prends soin de toi. 2/ Souhaite-moi bonne chance. 3/ Envoie-moi un email. 4/ Entends-tu un bruit ? 5/ Ne te décourage pas !

Exercise 15.7

1/ Donnez-moi un café, s'il vous plaît. 2/ Range ta chambre tout de suite. 3/ Passe-moi le sel. 4/ Fais tes devoirs avant de regarder la télé. 5/ N'oubliez pas d'apporter vos ordinateurs portables.

This book is awesome.

This book is more awesome than other books.

This book is the most awesome of all.

See? This book is so awesome that in three sentences it just illustrated the difference between comparative and superlative adjectives.

In both English and French, comparatives are used to compare superiority, inferiority, or equality between two or more things. As for the superlatives, we use it to talk about the extremes, like the worst or the best.

Since comparatives and superlatives are about description, they can occur both in adjectives and adverbs. We've listed the most important things you need to remember about comparatives and superlatives in French below.

1. First, for the adjectives:

Here are some tips and rules in using **comparative adjectives:**

- Use the French word **"plus"**, which means *"more"*.

  Example: Cette question est **plus** facile. *(This question is easier.)*

- Use the word **"moins"**, which means *"less"*.

  Example: Cette veste est **moins** chè**re.** *(This jacket is less expensive.)*

- Use the word **"que"** which means *"than"* when introducing the other person or thing you are comparing your subject with.

  Example: Elle est plus petite **que** moi. *(She's smaller than me.)*

- Use the word **"aussi"** paired with **"que"** to say your subject is similar to the other thing. In English, we use this to say, (subject) is as (adjective) as (subject 2).

  Example: Il est **aussi** inquiet **que** moi. *(He's as worried as me.)*

For **superlative adjectives**, here's a rundown of the things you should know:

- You can use **"plus"** to mean *"most"* depending on the form of the adjective you're using.

Masculine singular adjectives --- **le plus**

Feminine singular adjectives --- **la plus**

Plural adjectives (masculine and feminine) --- **les plus**

Examples:

- o le guide **le plus** utile *(the most useful guidebook)*
- o le question **la plus** facile *(the easiest question)*
- o **les plus** grands hôtels *(the biggest hotels)*

- You can use **"moins"** to mean *"least"* depending on the form of the adjective you're using.

Masculine singular adjectives --- **le moins**

Feminine singular adjectives --- **la moins**

Plural adjectives (masculine and feminine) --- **les moins**

Examples:

- o le guide **le moins** utile *(the least useful guidebook)*
- o le question **la moins** facile *(the least easy or the hardest question)*
- o les mois **les moins** agréables *(the least pleasant months)*

2. Now for the adverbs:

Comparatives and superlatives in adverbs work roughly the same way they do with adjectives. The main difference is that, unlike the adjectives, the superlatives of the adverbs no longer need to agree to the gender or number to the word they are describing (which makes life a lot easier, we must say).

Remember these tiny bits of information when using **comparative adverbs**:

- Use **"plus... que"** which means *"more... than"*.

  Example: Tu marches **plus** vite **que** moi. *(You walk faster than me.)*

- Use **"moins... que"** to say *"less... than"*.

  Example: Nous nous voyons **moins** souvent qu'avant. *(We now see each other less often than before.)*

- Use **"aussi... que"** to say *"as...as"*.

  Example: Je parle français **aussi** bien **que** toi! *(I can speak French as well as you!)*

For **superlative adverbs**, here are the things you should take note of:

- Superlatives in adverbs work the same way as they do in the adjectives, except for one thing: you no longer need to make **"le"** agree with the gender or number. In short, there is no **"la"** or **"les"** for the feminine and plural forms. **"Le"** stays as is.

- Use **"le plus"** to say *"the most"* or the *"_____-est"*.

    Example: **Michelle parle le plus vite.** *(Michelle speaks the fastest.)*

- Use **"le moins"** to say *"the least"* or the *"_____est"*.

    Example: **Cathy a mangé le moins.** *(Cathy ate the least.)*

LET'S PRACTICE!

Exercise 16.1

I. Comparatives:

Fill in the blank with the appropriate comparative of the adjective in parentheses. "+" is for "*more...than*", "-" for "*less...than*", and "=" for "*as...as*". Do not forget to make the adjectives agree in number and gender with the nouns they qualify.

1. L'anglais de Jean est _____ que celui de David. (+, mauvais)

    (John's English is ___ than David's.) (+, bad)

2. Julie a un _____ Q.I. ('I.Q.') que Sophie. (+, bon)

    (Julie has a ___ Q.I. ('I.Q.') than Sophie.) (+, good)

3. Sophie est _____ que Julie. (=, joli)

    (Sophie is ___ than Julie.) (=, pretty)

4. Luc est _____ que David. (+, gentil)

    (Luke is ___ than David.) (+, nice)

5. Les Spurs sont _____ que les Heat. (-, fort)

    (The Spurs are ___ than the Heat.) (-, strong)

II. Superlative

Fill in the blank with the appropriate superlative of the adjective in parentheses. "+" is for "*the most*", "-" for "*the least*". Do not forget to make the adjectives agree in number and gender with the nouns they qualify.

1. Jean a _____ accent de la classe. (+, mauvais)

    (John has ___ class accent.) (+, bad)

2. Le Q.I. ('I.Q.') de David est _____ de l'école. (+, bon)

    (David's Q.I. (I.Q.') is ___ from school.) (+, good)

3. Luna est la chatte _____ du campus. (+ mignonne)

    (Luna is the ___ campus cat.) (+ cute)

4. Sophie est l'employée _____ du magasin. (+, travailleur)

   (Sophie is the ____ store employee.) (+, worker)

5. Les singes sont les animaux _____ du zoo. (+, mignon)

   (Monkeys are the ____ animals of the zoo.) (+, cute)

6. Les vaches sont les animaux _____ de la ferme. (-, intelligent)

   (Cows are the ____ animals of the farm.) (-, clever)

Fun fact: French cuisine is considered one of the best in the world, and there are an average of two French cookery books being published every day in the world.

Exercise 16.2 - For each sentence, say whether the comparative or the superlative is used:

1. Je suis plus organisée que mon frère. *(I am more organized than my brother.)*

2. Tu es la personne la plus gentille que je connaisse. *(You're the kindest person I know.)*

3. Cet arbre est le plus vieux au monde. *(This tree is the oldest one in the world.)*

4. Il est aussi méchant que sa femme. *(He is as mean as his wife.)*

5. C'est le plus beau spectacle que j'ai jamais vu. *(It's the most beautiful show I've ever seen.)*

Exercise 16.3 - Complete these sentences with [plus], [moins] or [aussi]. Note: (+) is for superiority, (-) is for inferiority, and (=) is for equality:

1. Il est (=) _____ têtu que son frère. *(He's as stubborn as his brother.)*

2. Elle est (+) _____ grande que son petit copain. *(She's taller than her boyfriend.)*

3. Cette tâche est (-) _____ difficile que celle d'hier. *(This task is less difficult than the one from yesterday.)*

4. Ma chambre est (+) _____ grande que celle de ma sœur. *(My room is bigger than my sister's.)*

5. Il est (=) _____ séduisant que son père. *(He's as attractive as his father.)*

Exercise 16.4 - Complete these sentences with [le plus], [la plus] or [les plus]:

1. Marc est la personne _____ intelligente de la famille. *(Marc is the most intelligent person in the family).*

2. Je trouve que les chiots sont les animaux _____ mignons au monde. *(I think puppies are the cutest animals in the world.)*

3. Le petit-déjeuner est le repas _____ important de la journée. *(Breakfast is the most important meal of the day.)*

4. Joséphine est l'élève _____ brillante de la classe. *(Josephine is the brightest student in the class.)*

5. Léo est l'employé _____ sérieux du magasin. *(Leo is the most serious employee in the shop.)*

Exercise 16.5 - Complete these sentences with [plus], [moins], [aussi] or [que]:

1. Mon père est (+) _____ âgé _____ ma mère. *(My dad is older than my mother.)*

2. C'est le (+) _____ beau pays que j'ai visité. *(It's the most beautiful country I visited.)*

3. Il est (=) _____ maladroit _____ son fils. *(He's as clumsy as his son.)*

4. Ce livre est le (+) _____ intéressant que j'ai lu. *(This book is the most interesting one I've read.)*

5. Elle est la personne la (-) _____ paresseuse de la famille. *(She's the least lazy person of the family.)*

Exercise 16.6 - Use the words to create sentences:

Example: Marc/ (+) grand/ Léa ==> Marc est plus grand que Léa. *(Marc is taller than Lea.)*

1. Les chiens/ (+) mignons/ les chats. *(dogs/ (+) cute/ cats)*

   _____

2. La robe bleue/ (+) jolie/ la noire. *(The blue dress/ (+) pretty/ the black one)*

   _____

3. Le violon/ (-) facile à apprendre/ la guitare. *(Violin/ (-) easy to learn/ the guitar)*

_____

4. Marc/ (+) travailleur/ son meilleur ami. *(Marc/ (+) hardworking/ his bestfriend)*

_____

5. Julie/ (=) serviable/ sa sœur. *(Julie/ (=) helpful/ her sister)*

_____

Exercise 16.7 - Reorganize the words to make sentences:

Example : est l'élève la plus brillante/Marie/de sa classe ==> Marie est l'élève la plus brillante de sa classe. *(Marie is the brightest student in her class.)*

1. Ma mère/ que je connaisse/ est la personne la plus courageuse *(My mother/ that I know/ is the most courageous person.)*

_____

2. est l'élève le plus grand/de la classe/ Paul *(is the tallest student/ of the class/ Paul)*

_____

3. que j'ai jamais gouté/ C'est le gâteau/ le plus savoureux *(that I've ever tasted/ it's the cake/ the most delicious)*

_____

4. est le plus grand/ Ce bâtiment/ de la ville *(is the tallest/ This building/ in the city)*

_____

5. C'était l'étoile/ que j'aie jamais vue/ la plus brillante *(It was the star/ that I have ever seen/ the brightest)*

_____

ANSWERS:

Exercise 16.1
Track 45

I. Comparatives

1/ L'anglais de Jean est plus mauvais que celui de David. 2/ Julie a un meilleur Q.I. ('I.Q.') que Sophie. 3/ Sophie est aussi jolie que Julie. 4/ Luc est plus gentil que David. 5/ Les Spurs sont moins forts que les Heat.

II. Superlatives

1/ Jean a le plus mauvais accent de la classe. 2/ Le Q.I. ('I.Q.') de David est le meilleur de l'école. 3/ Luna est la chatte la plus mignonne du campus. 4/ Sophie est l'employée la plus travailleuse du magasin. 5/ Les singes sont les animaux les plus mignons du zoo. 6/ Les vaches sont les animaux les moins intelligents de la ferme.

Exercise 16.2

1/ Comparative 2/ Superlative 3/ Superlative 4/ Comparative 5/ Superlative

Exercise 16.3

1/ Il est aussi têtu que son frère. 2/ Elle est plus grande que son petit copain. 3/ Cette tâche est moins difficile que celle d'hier. 4/ Ma chambre est plus grande que celle de ma sœur. 5/ Il est aussi séduisant que son frère.

Exercise 16.4

1/ Marc est la personne la plus intelligente de la famille. 2/ Je trouve que les chiots sont les animaux les plus mignons au monde. 3/ Le petit-déjeuner est le repas le plus important de la journée. 4/ Joséphine est l'élève la plus brillante de la classe. 5/ Léo est l'employé le plus sérieux du magasin.

Exercise 16.5

1/ Mon père est plus âgé que ma mère. 2/ C'est le plus beau pays que j'ai visité. 3/ Il est aussi maladroit que son fils. 4/ Ce livre est le plus intéressant que j'ai lu. 5/ Elle est la personne la moins paresseuse de la famille.

Exercise 16.6

1/ Les chiens sont plus mignons que les chats. 2/ La robe bleue est plus jolie que la noire. 3/ Le violon est moins facile à apprendre que la guitare. 4/ Marc est plus travailleur que son meilleur ami. 5/ Julie est aussi serviable que sa sœur.

Exercise 16.7

1/ Ma mère est la personne la plus courageuse que je connaisse. 2/ Paul est l'élève le plus grand de la classe. 3/ C'est le gâteau le plus savoureux que j'ai jamais gouté. 4/ Ce bâtiment est le plus grand de la ville. 5/ C'était l'étoile la plus brillante que j'aie jamais vue.

DAY 17
POSSESSIVE AND DEMONSTRATIVE ADJECTIVES

We all know what adjectives can do (right?) These are the words that describe a noun. But their purpose is not limited to descriptions such as "cool" or "kind" or "pretty". They have a host of other uses, such as providing more information about the noun they're appearing with, or even pointing out something.

In this lesson, we'll be talking about (or rather, breezing through) **possessive adjectives** and **demonstrative adjectives**. These are relatively easy topics that won't be needing a lot of brain cell activity. So, sit back and try to enjoy today's topic.

First, **possessive adjectives**:

When you need to express that a noun belongs to another person or thing, you use possessive adjectives. We know it in English as the words: *my, your, his, her, its, our,* and *their*.

In French, the possessive adjectives (like all other kinds of adjectives) need to agree with the noun they're describing.

Here's a nifty little table to cover all that.

Track 46

When used with masculine singular noun	When used with feminine singular noun	When used with plural noun whether feminine or masculine	What it means
mon	ma (*mon)	mes	*my*
ton	ta (*ton)	tes	*your*
son	sa (*son)	ses	*his/her/its/one's*
notre	notre	nos	*our*
votre	votre	vos	*your*
leur	leur	leurs	*their*

*Note that **mon, ton** and **son** are used in the feminine form with nouns that begin with a vowel or the letter "**h**".

Here are some more reminders in using possessive adjectives:

- Possessive adjectives always come BEFORE the noun.

- Possessive adjectives don't "agree" with the owner of the item being used in the sentence, but with the item itself.

- In French, possessive adjectives are not used to point out body parts. **Le, la l'** or **les** are being used instead (don't ask us why!).

Exercise 17.1 - Choose the correct answer:

1. ___ soeur est gentille. *(My sister is kind.)*

   a. Ma   b. Mon   c. Mes

2. J'aime ___ chien. *(I love my dog.)*

   a. ta   b. sa   c. mon

3. J'ai ouvert ___ armoire. *(I opened my wardrobe.)*

   a. mon   b. ma   c. ton

4. Prends ___ voiture. *(Take your car.)*

   a. ma   b. ta   c. ton

5. J'ai oublié ___ clés. *(I forgot my keys.)*

   a. mon   b. ma   c. mes

Exercise 17.2 - Fill in the blanks with [mon], [ma] or [mes]:

1. _____ voiture est tombée en panne. *(My car broke down.)*

2. Il a mangé _____ yaourt. *(He ate my yogurt.)*

3. J'ai perdu _____ lunettes. *(I lost my glasses.)*

4. Ils m'ont acheté un délicieux gâteau pour _____ anniversaire. *(They bought me a delicious cake for my birthday.)*

5. _____ jambes me font mal après l'entraînement. *(My legs hurt after the workout.)*

Exercise 17.3 - Fill in the blanks with [ton], [ta], or [tes]:

1. Tu as oublié _____ cahier. *(You forgot your notebook.)*

2. J'ai pris _____ parapluie. *(I took your umbrella.)*

3. As-tu fais _____ devoirs ? *(Did you do your homework?)*

4. Puis-je emprunter _____ calculatrice ? *(May I borrow you calculator?)*

5. Il a vraiment apprécié _____ aide. *(He really appreciated your help.)*

Exercise 17.4 - Fill in the blanks with [son], [sa], or [ses]:

1. J'adore _____ robe. Elle lui va bien. *(I love her dress. It suits her well.)*

2. Il a oublié _____ manteau chez moi. *(He forgot his coat at my place.)*

3. J'aime beaucoup _____ sourire. *(I like her smile a lot.)*

4. Il est allé voir un film avec _____ amis. *(He went to see a movie with his friends.)*

5. Il a acheté un cadeau pour _____ mère. *(He bought a gift for his mom.)*

Exercise 17.5 - Fill in the blanks with notre, [nos], [votre], [vos], [leur], or [leurs]:

1. Vous avez une belle maison. J'adore particulièrement _____ jardin. *(You have a nice house. I particularly like your garden.)*

2. Jeanne et Patrick emmènent _____ fils au parc chaque jour. *(Jeanne and Patrick take their son to the park every day.)*

3. Nous allons avoir un repas de Noël avec _____ grands-parents. *(We're going to have a Christmas meal with our grandparents.)*

4. Pouvez-vous retirez _____ chaussures ? *(Can you take off your shoes?)*

5. Ils mettent _____ valises dans la voiture. *(They put their suitcases in the car.)*

With those exercises out of the way, let's move on to the next topic: **demonstrative adjectives**.

Here are some things to fill you in about **demonstrative adjectives**:

- Demonstrative adjectives are used to point out something. In English, these are the words: *"this"*, *"that"*, *"these"*, and *"those"* (e.g., this book, that face, *these goosebumps*, and *those creatures*.)

- In French, the word **"ce"** covers demonstrative adjectives in its entirety. This will, however, change its form depending on the kind of noun.

Singular masculine – **ce (cet*)**

Singular feminine – **cette**

Both mean **this** or **that**.

Plural masculine – **ces**

Plural feminine – **ces**

Both mean **these** or **those**.

"cet" is used for singular masculine nouns that begin with either a *vowel* or a *h*.

- Important items to remember when using **"ce"**:

  1. **"ce"** always comes BEFORE the noun it is referring to, no matter what its form is.

  2. **"-ci"** is added at the end of the noun to point out its nearness to you. **"-là"** is added at the end of the noun to point out that it is far from you.

  Track 47

  Example:

  - **Prends cette valise-ci.** *(Take this case.)*
  - **Est-ce que tu reconnais cette personne-là ?** *(Do you recognize that person?)*

...and with that we're done for the day. (Hooray!)

But wait, here are some more exercises.

Exercise 17.6 - Fill in the blanks with [ce], [cet], [cette], or [ces]:

1. _____ appartement est spacieux. *(This apartment is spacious.)*

2. J'aime la couleur de ___rideaux. *(I love the color of these curtains.)*

3. J'ai vu ___groupe de musique en concert la semaine dernière. *(I saw this band in concert last week.)*

4. ___banane est délicieuse. *(This banana is delicious.)*

5. Sandra a commencé à faire du sport ___dernières années. *(Sandra started working out these last years.)*

LET'S PRACTICE SOME MORE!

Exercise 17.7

I. Possessive Adjectives - Fill in the blanks with the correct possessive adjective.

1. _____ famille est intéressante. *(my)* (__ *family is interesting).*

2. _____ neveux sont ici. *(your)* (__ *nephews are here).*

3. Jean, David et Julie sont _____ amis. *(my)* (*Jean, David and Julie are* __ *friends.)*

4. _____ amour est éternel. *(their)* (__ *love is eternal.)*

5. _____visite me fait plaisir. *(your)* (__ *visit makes me happy.)*

II. Demonstrative Adjectives - Fill in the blank with the correct demonstrative adjective: [ce], [cet], [cette], or [ces].

1. Tu as vu le film _____ matin ? *(Did you see the movie* __ *morning?)*

2. Je suis folle de ('crazy about') _____ animal ! *(I'm crazy about* __ *animal!)*

3. Qui est _____ jolie fille ? *(Who is* __ *pretty girl?)*

4. Que faites-vous _____ après-midi ? *(What are you doing* __ *afternoon?)*

5. _____ enfants sont naïfs ! (__ *children are naive!)*

Fun fact: The first Wednesday of every month in France, a war siren is sounded as a drill. If the alarm sounds on a day other than Wednesday, that means France is at war from that moment on.

Exercise 17.8 - Fill in the blanks with the correct possessive adjective:

1. J'adore _____ nouvelle coupe de cheveux. Ça te va bien. *(I love your new haircut. It suits you well.)*

2. Le chien de mon frère adore _____ balle de tennis. *(My brother's dog loves his tennis ball.)*

3. _____ parents me donnent _____ argent de poche chaque semaine. *(My parents give me my pocket money every week.)*

4. Jonathan porte _____ chaussures. *(Jonathan wears his shoes.)*

5. Camille offre un cadeau à _____ mère pour _____ anniversaire. *(Camille offers a gift to her mother for her birthday.)*

Exercise 17.9 - Fill in the blanks with the correct demonstrative adjective:

1. _____ petits chiots sont très mignons. *(These little puppies are very cute.)*

2. Aidez-moi à porter _____ armoire. *(Help me carry this wardrobe.)*

3. _____ arbre a été planté par mon grand-père. *(This tree has been planted by my grandfather.)*

4. Ça fait une heure que je suis coincé dans _____ embouteillage. *(It has been an hour that I've been stuck in this traffic jam.)*

5. Peux-tu attacher _____ guirlandes, s'il te plaît ? *(Can you attach these garlands please?)*

ANSWERS:

Exercise 17.1

1/ ma 2/ mon 3/ mon 4/ ta 5/ mes

Exercise 17.2

1/ Ma voiture est tombée en panne. 2/ Il a mangé mon yaourt. 3/ J'ai perdu mes lunettes. 4/ Ils m'ont acheté un délicieux gâteau pour mon anniversaire. 5/ Mes jambes me font mal après l'entraînement.

Exercise 17.3

1/ Tu as oublié ton cahier. 2/ J'ai pris ton parapluie. 3/ As-tu fais tes devoirs ? 4/ Puis-je emprunter ta calculatrice ? 5/ Il a vraiment apprécié ton aide.

Exercise 17.4

1/ J'adore sa robe. Elle lui va bien. 2/ Il a oublié son manteau chez moi. 3/ J'aime beaucoup son sourire. 4/ Il est allé voir un film avec ses amis. 5/ Il a acheté un cadeau pour sa mère.

Exercise 17.5

1/ Vous avez une belle maison. J'adore particulièrement votre jardin. 2/ Jeanne et Patrick emmènent leur fils au parc chaque jour. 3/ Nous allons avoir un repas de Noël avec nos grands-parents. 4/ Pouvez-vous retirez vos chaussures ? 5/ Ils mettent leurs valises dans la voiture.

Exercise 17.6

1/ Cet appartement est spacieux. 2/ J'aime la couleur de ces rideaux. 3/ J'ai vu ce groupe de musique en concert la semaine dernière. 4/ Cette banane est délicieuse. 5/ Sandra a commencé à faire du sport ces dernières années.

Exercise 17.7
Track 48
I. Possessive Adjectives

1/ Ma famille est intéressante. (my) 2/ Vos neveux sont ici. (your) 3/ Jean, David et Julie sont mes amis. (my) 4/ Leur amour est éternel. (their) 5/ Votre visite me fait plaisir (your)

II. Demonstrative Adjectives

1/ Tu as vu le film ce matin ? 2/ Je suis folle de ('crazy about') cet animal !
3/ Qui est cette jolie fille ? 4/ Que faites-vous cet (or cette) après-midi?
5/ Ces enfants sont naïfs !

Exercise 17.8

1/ J'adore ta nouvelle coupe de cheveux. Ça te va bien. 2/ Le chien de mon frère adore sa balle de tennis. 3/ Mes parents me donnent mon argent de poche chaque semaine. 4/ Jonathan porte ses chaussures. 5/ Camille offre un cadeau à sa mère pour son anniversaire.

Exercise 17.9

1/ Ces petits chiots sont très mignons. 2/ Aidez-moi à porter cette armoire.
3/ Cet arbre a été planté par mon grand-père. 4/ Ça fait une heure que je suis coincé dans cet embouteillage. 5/ Peux-tu attacher ces guirlandes, s'il te plaît?

By now you are probably already aware of why pronouns were put upon this earth: they stand in place of nouns. Nouns can either be the subject or the object of a sentence, and pronouns, being the stand-in for the nouns, can also be both.

Enter the direct object and indirect object pronouns.

So which is which, and how do you know if it's direct or indirect?

- **Direct objects** are the persons or things that are the receiver of the action in the sentence.

- **Direct objects** answer the question "*who*" or "*what*".

  Example:

  - *I ate a sandwich.* The <u>sandwich</u> is the direct object.
  - *I ate it.* <u>It</u> is the direct object pronoun.

- **Indirect objects** are persons or things to whom or for whom the action occurs.

- **Indirect objects** are introduced by the preposition "*to*" and "*for*". It answers the question *to whom/for whom* or *to what/for what*.

  Example:

  - *I sang a song for the crowd.* The <u>crowd</u> is the indirect object.
  - *I sang them a song.* <u>Them</u> is the indirect object pronoun.

Now, let's take a look at **direct object pronouns** in detail.

Here are the different direct object pronouns in French and their corresponding meanings in English.

1. **"me"** (or **m'** in front of a vowel or mute **-h**) – This also means "*me*".

2. **"te"** (or **t'** in front of a vowel or mute-**h**) – This means "*you*" (second person singular – and used in talking to someone familiar to you or informally)

3. **"le"** (or **l'** in front of a vowel or mute-**h**) – This means "*him/it*" (third person singular – masculine)

4. **"la"** (or **l'** in front of a vowel or mute **-h**) – This means "*her/it*" (third person singular – feminine)

5. **"nous"** – This means "*us*".

6. **"vous"** – This means *"you"*. Used for formal speech in the singular, or for both informal and formal speech in plural.

7. **"les"** – This means *"them"*.

Remember: Because the pronouns stand in for the noun, you select the pronoun based on the gender and number of the noun you are replacing with it.

For example: **la mère** *(the mother)* is a singular feminine noun, so it should be replaced with the direct object pronoun **"la"**.

Example:

- o **Je vois ma mère.** *(I see my mother.)*
- o **Je la vois.** *(I see her.)*

Direct object pronouns appear BEFORE the verb.

Now, let's meet the indirect object pronouns and their English counterparts.

1. **"me"** (or **m'** in front of a vowel or mute **-h**) – This means *"me"* or *"to me"*.

2. **"te"** (or **t'** in front of a vowel or mute **-h**) – This means "you" or *"to you"*, and is used for singular informal speech.

3. **"lui"** – This means *"him/her"* or *"to him/to her"*.

4. **"nous"** – This means *"us"* or "to *us*".

5. **"vous"** – This means *"you"* or "to you", and is used in singular formal or plural formal and informal speech.

6. **"leur"** – This means *"them"* or *"to them"*.

Remember the following:

- Indirect object pronouns are similar to the direct object pronouns except for the third person singular and plural. Both *"him"* and *"her"* are **"lui"** in French, with no distinction between genders. Additionally, the third person plural is **"leur"**, regardless of the gender of the noun being replaced.

- Just like the direct object pronouns, indirect object pronouns usually appear before the verb.

  Example:

  - o **Il parle aux fantômes.** *(He speaks to ghosts.)*
  - o **Il leur parle.** *(He speaks to them.)*

In French, indirect object pronouns are used only for objects that are sentient (human or animals). For things, the adverbial pronoun **"y"** is used instead.

LET'S PRACTICE!

Exercise 18.1 - Select the right answer from the choices given:

1. Vous _____achetez ? (it) *(Are you buying it?)*

   l'? / les? / le? / la?

2. Tu _____vois ? (her) *(Can you see her?)*

   la? / elle? / lui? / le?

3. Je _____aime beaucoup. (them) *(I like them a lot.)*

   leur? / l'? / leurs? / les?

4. Je cherche mon stylo, (it) _____était sur mon bureau. *(I'm looking for my pen. It was on my desk.)*

   ce? /c'? / elle? / il?

5. Elle _____demande de l'aider. (them) *(She is asking them to help her.)*

   leurs? / lui? / les? / leur?

> ***Fun fact:*** In French New Year celebrations, there is a cake called " galette de rois " which is made of puff pastry, flour, egg, rum and almond paste. A small ceramic lucky charm is hidden in each cake. When family members share the cake, whoever finds the little gift in their slice is the lucky one.

Exercise 18.2 - Say if the underlined group of words is a direct object or an indirect object:

1. J'aime <u>le fromage.</u> *(I like cheese.)*

2. Elle a entendu <u>son chien</u> aboyer. *(She heard her dog barking.)*

3. J'ai donné les clés à <u>Sandra.</u> *(I gave the keys to Sandra.)*

4. Tu peux prendre <u>mon stylo.</u> *(You can take my pen.)*

5. Il est allé à la fête pour faire plaisir à <u>sa femme.</u> *(He went to the party to please his wife.)*

Exercise 18.3 - Replace the underlined group of words with the correct direct object pronoun and rewrite the sentence:

1. Je mange <u>des fruits.</u> (*I eat some fruit.*)

   _____

2. Il a oublié <u>son manteau</u>. (*He forgot his coat.*)

   _____

3. J'ai passé <u>mon examen</u> avec succès. (*I passed my exam with success.*)

   _____

4. Claire amènera <u>sa voiture</u> pour nous chercher. (*Claire will bring her car to pick us up.*)

   _____

5. Lucien est allé rejoindre <u>ses amis</u> dans la cafétéria. (*Lucien went to join his friends in the cafeteria.*)

   _____

Exercise 18.4 - Fill in the blanks with [me], [te], [le], [la], [l'], [nous], [vous], or [les]:

1. Je te conseille d'acheter cette crème hydratante. Je _____ utilise souvent et je trouve que c'est un bon produit. (*I advise you to buy this moisturizer. I use it often, and I think it's a good product.*)

2. Nous avons eu un très bon serveur. Il _____ a apporté notre commande rapidement et avec le sourire. (*We had a very good server. He brought us our order quickly and with a smile.*)

3. Je vais aller au musée du Louvre avec Benoît. Il va _____ montrer la fameuse Joconde. (*I am going to go to the Louvre Museum with Benoit. He's going to show me the famous Mona Lisa.*)

4. As-tu reçu le colis ? Je _____ ai envoyé mardi dernier. (*Did you recieved the package? I sent it last Tuesday.*)

5. Où sont mes lunettes ? Je _____ ai cherchées partout. (*Where are my glasses? I looked for them everywhere.*)

Exercise 18.5 - Complete the sentences with the correct direct object pronouns:

1. J'ai adoré ce film. Je _____ ai vu la semaine dernière. *(I loved this movie. I saw it last week.)*

2. Il a pris ton parapluie. Il te _____ rendra demain. *(He took your umbrealla. He will give it back to you tomorrow.)*

3. Il habite dans mon quartier. Je _____ vois chaque matin en allant au travail. *(He lives in my neighborhood. I see him every morning on my way to work.)*

4. Mon chien est très énergique. Il _____ fait rire quand il court partout dans la maison. *(My dog is very energetic. He makes me laugh when he runs all around the house.)*

5. Il va voir avec son supérieur et il _____ rappellera. *(He will see with his supervisor and he will call us back.)*

Exercise 18.6 - Fill in the blanks with [me], [te], [lui], [nous], [vous], [leur], or [y]:

1. Notre chien a toujours faim. Ma sœur _____ donne souvent à manger. *(Our dog is always hungry. My sister often gives him food.)*

2. J'adore ce restaurant. J'_____ vais une fois par mois. *(I love this restaurant. I go to it once per month.)*

3. Le professeur _____ rend nos copies d'examen. *(The professor returns us our copies of the exam.)*

4. Va à la bibliothèque. Nous _____ rejoindrons plus tard. *(Go to the library. We will join you later.)*

5. Je suis impatient d'aller chez ma mère ce week-end. Elle va _____ préparer mon plat préféré. *(I'm excited to go to my mom's this weekend. She will prepare my favorite dish for me.)*

Exercise 18.7 - Replace the underlined group of words with the correct indirect pronoun and rewrite the sentence:

1. J'ai envoyé une lettre <u>à mon ami.</u> *(I sent a letter to my friend.)*

   _____

2. Robert aime dire des blagues <u>à ses collègues</u>. *(Robert likes telling jokes to his colleagues.)*

_____

3. J'ai fait un câlin <u>à ma mère</u>. *(I gave a hug to my mother.)*

_____

4. Ils sont partis regarder un match de football <u>au stade</u>. *(They went to see a game of football at the stadium.)*

_____

5. Il souhaite un joyeux Noël <u>à toi et tes parents</u>. *(He wishes a merry Christmas to you and your parents.)*

_____

Exercise 18.8 - Complete the sentences with the correct indirect object pronouns:

1. Les étudiants entrent dans la salle. Le prof _____ rend leurs copies. *(The students enter the classroom. The teacher gives them their copies.)*

2. J'aime ma grand-mère. Je _____ rends visite au moins une fois par semaine. *(I love my grandma. I visit her at least once a week.)*

3. Mon petit frère _____ prend la main et _____ 'emmène dehors pour voir la neige. *(My little brother is taking my hand and taking me outside to see the snow.)*

4. Il ___ prête la voiture à condition de la _____ rendre avant midi. *(He is lending you the car on condition that you give it back to him before noon.)*

5. Peux-tu _____ rappeler cet après-midi ? *(Can you call me back this afternoon?)*

Exercise 18.9 - Replace the underlined group of words with the correct pronouns and rewrite the sentence:

1. Je donne <u>mes clés</u> <u>à mon petit ami.</u> *(I give my keys to my boyfriend.)*

_____

2. Il envoie <u>le ballon</u> <u>à ses enfants</u>. *(He sends the ball to his children.)*

_____

3. J'ai promis à <u>ma mère</u> <u>de prendre soin de son poisson</u>. *(I promised my mother to take care of her fish.)*

_____

4. Je passe <u>ma carte bancaire</u> <u>à la caissière</u>. *(I am passing my credit card to the cashier.)*

_____

5. Sabine prête <u>sa boussole</u> <u>à Claude et Jamy</u> pour leur excursion. *(Sabine is lending her compass to Claude and Jamy for their excursion.)*

_____

ANSWERS:

Exercise 18.1
Track 49

1/ Vous l'achetez ? 2/ Tu la vois ? 3/ Je les aime beaucoup. 4/ Je cherche mon stylo, il/ c'était sur mon bureau. 5/ Elle leur demande de l'aider.

Exercise 18.2

1/ A direct object 2/ A direct object 3/ An indirect object 4/ A direct object 5/ An indirect object

Exercise 18.3

1/ Je les mange. 2/ Il l'a oublié. 3/ Je l'ai passé avec succès. 4/ Claire l'amènera pour nous chercher. 5/ Lucien est allé les rejoindre dans la cafétéria.

Exercise 18.4

1/ Je te conseille d'acheter cette crème hydratante. Je l'utilise souvent et je trouve que c'est un bon produit. 2/ Nous avons eu un très bon serveur. Il nous a apporté notre commande rapidement et avec le sourire. 3/ Je vais aller au musée du Louvre avec Benoît. Il va me montrer la fameuse Joconde. 4/ As-tu reçu le colis? Je l'ai envoyé mardi dernier. 5/ Où sont mes lunettes ? Je les ai cherchées partout.

Exercise 18.5

1/ J'ai adoré ce film. Je l'ai vu la semaine dernière. 2/ Il a pris ton parapluie. Il te le rendra demain. 3/ Il habite dans mon quartier. Je le vois chaque matin en allant au travail. 4/ Mon chien est très énergique. Il me fait rire quand il court partout dans la maison. 5/ Il va voir avec son supérieur et il nous rappellera.

Exercise 18.6

1/ Notre chien a toujours faim. Ma soeur lui donne souvent à manger. 2/ J'adore ce restaurant. J'y vais une fois par mois. 3/ Le professeur nous rend nos copies d'examen. 4/ Va à la bibliothèque. Nous te rejoindrons plus tard. 5/ Je suis impatient d'aller chez ma mère ce week-end. Elle va me préparer mon plat préféré.

Exercise 18.7

1/ Je lui ai envoyé une lettre. 2/ Robert aime leur dire des blagues. 3/ Je lui ai fait un câlin. 4/ Ils y sont partis regarder un match de football. 5/ Il vous souhaite un joyeux Noël.

Exercise 18.8

1/ Les étudiants entrent dans la salle. Le prof leur rend leurs copies. 2/ J'aime ma grand-mère. Je lui rends visite au moins une fois par semaine. 3/ Mon petit frère me prend la main et m'emmène dehors pour voir la neige. 4/ Il te prête la voiture à condition de la lui rendre avant midi. 5/ Peux-tu me rappeler cet après-midi ?

Exercise 18.9

1/ Je les lui donne. 2/ Il le leur envoie. 3/ Je le lui ai promis. 4/ Je la lui passe. 5/ Sabine la leur prête pour leur excursion.

DAY 19
THE SUBJUNCTIVE MOOD

(and a little Q&A about it)

French subjunctive? What is it? If this is the first time you've heard of such a thing, don't worry. You're not alone.

Question number 1: What exactly is it?

The **subjunctive** is a grammatical mood which can be found in different languages, including English and French. However, it is much more widely used in French than English.

- The subjunctive is used to **express varied states of unreality or uncertainty** - such as a judgment, wish, possibility, opinion, doubt, emotion, or something that has not yet occurred.

- You need to remember two things when it comes to what the subjunctive means:

  SUBJECTIVITY and UNREALITY. If it can't be classified as either, you usually make use of the indicative mood.

- What's weird is, there is no future tense in the subjunctive, only past and present. If it is set to happen in the future, the present tense is used once again.

Question number 2: What is the subjunctive like in English?

- We use it when we say things like "*If I _were_ you*" or "*It is important that he _stop_ to read the signs*", and other similar subjective statements.

- The subjunctive often appears in subordinate clauses especially *that-clauses*.

Question number 3: When and where do you use it?

- In French, we use the subjunctive after certain words and conjunctions that have two parts and two different subjects.

  Example: **Nous voulons qu'elle soit heureuse.** *(We want her to be happy.)* The first part of the sentence uses nous as the subject, while the second part uses **"elle"**. Therefore, the subjunctive **"soit"** is used.

- The subjunctives usually appear after these verb types:

Track 50

Wishing something:

- o **vouloir que** and **désirer que** (which means *"to wish that"* or *"to want"*), **aimer que** (meaning *"to like that"*)
- o **aimer mieux que** and **préférer que** (which means to *"prefer that"*).

Fearing something:

- o **avoir peur que** (which means to be *"afraid that"*).

Giving your opinion:

- o **croire que** (which means *"to think that"*).

Saying *"how you feel"*:

- o **regretter que** (meaning *"to be sorry that"*).
- o **être content que** (meaning *"to be pleased that"*).
- o **être surpris que** (meaning *"to be surprised that"*), etc.

- The subjunctive may also appear in some expressions that begin with **"il"**.

Some examples:

- o **il faut que** (*it is necessary that*)
- o **il vaut mieux que** (*it is better that*)

Question number 4: How do you form the subjunctive?

- For verbs that end with **-er**, here is how you form the subjunctive: **INFINITIVE minus -ER plus CORRECT ENDING.**

These are the endings to be added, depending on the pronoun it is being used with.

- For **je (j')**, add the ending **-e** (example: je donne)
- For **tu**, add the ending **-es** (example: tu donnes)
- For **il, elle,** or **on**, add the ending **-e** (examples: il donne, elle donne, on donne)
- For **nous**, add the ending **-ions** (example: nous donnions)
- For **vous**, add the ending **-iez** (example: vous donniez)
- For **ils** or **elles**, add the ending **-ent** (examples: ils donnent, elles donnent)

- For verbs that end with **-ir**, **INFINITIVE minus -IR plus CORRECT ENDING.**

  These are the endings to be added:

  - For **je (j')**, add the ending **-isse** (example: je finisse)

  - For **tu**, add the ending **-isses** (example: tu finisses)

  - For **il**, **elle**, or **on**, add the ending **-isse** (examples: il finisse, elle finisse, on finisse)

  - For **nous**, add the ending **-issions** (example: nous finissions)

  - For **vous**, add the ending **-issiez** (example: vous finissiez)

  - For **ils** or elles, add the ending **-issent** (examples: ils finissent, elles finissent)

- For verbs that end with **-re**, the subjunctive is formed by following this guide: **INFINITIVE minus -RE plus CORRECT ENDING.** The endings are the same as thosewith the **-er** verbs.

LET'S PRACTICE!

Exercise 19.1 - Select the right answer from the choices given:

1. Je veux que tu (savoir) _____ la vérité. (*I want you to know the truth.*)

   saves? / savais? / saches? / sais?

2. Bien que je (avoir) ____ mis un pull, j'ai toujours froid. (*Although I've put a jumper on, I'm still cold.*)

   aies? / avez? / ai? / aie?

3. Il vaut mieux que tu (porter) _____ un costume. (*It would be better if you wore a suit.*)

   portais? / portez? / portes? / porte?

4. Il est important que tu y (aller) _____ tout de suite. (*It is important that you leave right away.*)

   vailles? / iras? / vas? / ailles?

5. Ils veulent que je (ranger) _____ ma chambre. (*They want me to tidy my room.*)

   range? / rangez? / ranges? / rangie?

> ***Fun fact:*** Horse meat, frog's legs and snails are delicacies for the French.

Exercise 19.2: Conjugate "être" (to be), "avoir" (to have), and "aller" (to go) in the subjunctive:

	être	avoir	aller
que je			
que tu			
qu'il/elle			
que nous			
que vous			
qu'ils/elles			

Exercise 19.3 - Choose the correct answer:

1. Il faut qu'elle ___ courageuse. *(She must be brave.)*

   a. soit   b. est   c. soient

2. Je préfère que tu ___ chercher ma mère. *(I prefer that you go get my mom.)*

   a. vas   b. aille   c. ailles

3. Elle veut que je ___ des cours d'anglais. *(She wants me to take English classes.)*

   a. pris   b. prenne   c. prennes

4. Il faut que vous me ___. *(You have to believe me.)*

   a. croyiez   b. croyez   c. croie

5. Il souhaite que je ___ maintenant. *(He wishes me to leave now.)*

   a. préfère   b. préfères   c. préfèrent

Exercise 19.4 - Conjugate these verbs in the subjunctive:

1. Je veux que tu (savoir) _____ la vérité. *(I want you to know the truth.)*

2. Il est important que tu (sourire) _____ aux clients. *(It is important that you smile at the clients.)*

3. Il faut que je (nourrir) _____ mon chien avant de partir. *(I have to feed my dog before leaving.)*

4. Il veut que nous (faire) _____ nos devoirs avant de regarder la télé. *(He wants us to do our homework before watching TV.)*

5. Elle est contente que son fils (aider) _____ son père avec les travaux. *(She is pleased that her son helps his father with the work.)*

Exercise 19.5 - Conjugate "manger" (to eat), "partir" (to leave), and "croire" (to believe) in the subjunctive:

	manger	partir	croire
que je			
que tu			
qu'il/elle			
que nous			
que vous			
qu'ils/elles			

Exercise 19.6 - Conjugate these verbs in the subjunctive:

1. Il faut que tu (faire) _____ de ton mieux. *(You need to do your best.)*

2. Je veux que nous (être) _____ d'accord sur la couleur de la chambre. *(I want us to agree on the color of the room.)*

3. Faut-il que je (sortir) _____ après la réception ? *(Do I have to go out after the reception?)*

4. Il ne tolère pas que vous (parler) _____ si fort. *(He doesn't tolerate that you talk so loudly.)*

5. Il ne voit pas très bien, il faut qu'il (mettre) _____ ses lunettes. *(He doesn't see very well. He must put on his glasses.)*

ANSWERS:

Exercise 19.1
Track 51

1/ Je veux que tu saches la vérité. 2/ Bien que j'aie mis un pull, j'ai toujours froid. 3/ Il vaut mieux que tu portes un costume. 4/ Il est important que tu y ailles tout de suite. 5/ Ils veulent que je range ma chambre.

Exercise 19.2

	être	**avoir**	**aller**
que je	sois	aie	aille
que tu	sois	aies	ailles
qu'il/elle	soit	ait	aille
que nous	soyons	ayons	allions
que vous	soyez	ayez	alliez
qu'ils/elles	soient	aient	aillent

Exercise 19.3

1/ soit 2/ ailles 3/ prenne 4/ croyiez 5/ parte

Exercise 19.4

1/ Je veux que tu saches la vérité. 2/ Il est important que tu souries aux clients. 3/ Il faut que je nourrisse mon chien avant de partir. 4/ Il veut que nous fassions nos devoirs avant de regarder la télé. 5/ Elle est contente que son fils aide son père avec les travaux.

Exercise 19.5

	manger	**partir**	**croire**
que je	mange	parte	croie
que tu	manges	partes	croies
qu'il/elle	mange	parte	croie
que nous	mangions	partions	croyions
que vous	mangiez	partiez	croyiez
qu'ils/elles	mangent	partent	croient

Exercise 19.6

1/ Il faut que tu fasses de ton mieux. 2/ Je veux que nous soyons d'accord sur la couleur de la chambre. 3/ Faut-il que je sorte après la réception ? 4/ Il ne tolère pas que vous parliez si fort. 5/ Il ne voit pas très bien, il faut qu'il mette ses lunettes.

DAY 20
CONDITIONALS

You use conditionals, I use conditionals, all of us do – whether deliberately or not. It's ingrained in our daily speech, in either English or French.

So what is it, you ask?

It's a form of verb that we use when talking about things that may happen under certain conditions. In English we simply use the modal verbs "*would*" or "*could*" or its shortened form **-'d**, and then we add the main verb after it.

For example: *I would buy a new car if I had enough money.*

You wish it would be that easy in French, but it isn't.

First, let's look at the other **uses of the conditional**:

- To **ask politely** or formally, especially in public settings.

  Example*: I would like a cup of coffee, please.*

- To **say what you would like or need**.

  Example: *I would like to live in a house like this.*

- To **make a suggestion**.

  Example: *I could come over and cheer you up.*

- To **give advice to someone**.

  Example: *You should tell him you're sorry.*

- To **play roles, imaginary or not**.

  Example: *I would be the doctor and you would be the nurse.*

- To **nag or complain**.

  Example: *You could clean your room instead of sleeping around all day.*

- In "**even if**" or "**in case of**" clauses.

  Example: *Even if he were to sleep all day, he'd still get good grades.*

The basic rules:

- Most verbs in the conditional form follow this format: the infinitive (used as the stem) + an ending similar to that of the endings for the imperfect tense: **-ais, -ais, -ait, -ions, -iez,** and **-aient.**

- To put it simply, INFINITIVE + IMPERFECT TENSE ENDING equals a conditional form.

For example:

donner (*to give*) becomes:

Track 52

- o **Je donnerais**
- o **Tu donnerais**
- o **Il/elle/on donnerait**
- o **Nous donnerions**
- o **Vous donneriez**
- o **Ils/ elles donneraient**

finir (*to finish*) becomes:

Track 53

- o **Je finirais**
- o **Tu finirais**
- o **Il/elle/on finirait**
- o **Nous finirions**
- o **Vous finiriez**
- o **Ils/ elles finiraient**

Some changes in spelling for the conditional stem of regular **-er** verbs:

- The consonants '**l**' and '**t**' in those verbs which end in **-eler** and **-eter** are doubled. The pronunciation of the first letter **e** also changes from "**uhr**" to "**eh**". Exceptions are the words **geler** (*to freeze*), **peler** (*to peel*) and **acheter** (*to buy*).

Example:

appeler *(to call)* becomes:

Track 54

- o J'appellerais
- o Tu appellerais
- o Il / elle / on appellerait
- o Nous appellerions
- o Vous appelleriez
- o Ils / Elles appelleraient

- For verbs that end in -**yer**, the **"y"** often becomes **"i"** when used in the future tense.
  Example:
  nettoyer (*to clean*) becomes:

Track 55

- o Je nettoierais
- o Tu nettoierais
- o Il / elle/ on nettoierait
- o Nous nettoierions
- o Vous nettoieriez
- o Ils / elles nettoieraient

LET'S PRACTICE!

Exercise 20.1 - Choose the right form of the connector in brackets from the choices given:

1. Si nous avions de l'argent, nous (donner) _____ à la Croix-Rouge.

   (If we had any money, we would give to the Red Cross.)

   donneriont? / donneront? / donnerons? / donnerions?

2. Nous (aimer) _____ vous voir plus souvent.

   (We'd like to see you more often.)

   aimeriont? / aimerons? / aimeriez? / aimerions?

3. Si tu m'aidais, je (finir) _____ ce travail plus vite.

   (If you helped me I'd finish this job more quickly.)

   finirait? / finirai? / finira? / finirais?

4. S'il n'était pas si cher, je (commander) _____ ce manteau.

   (If it wasn't so expensive, I would order this coat.)

   commanderait? / commanderiez? / commanderais? / commanderaient?

5. S'il n'était pas fatigué, je lui (demander) _____ de m'aider.

   (If he wasn't tired, I'd ask him to help me.)

   demanderais? / demandera? / demanderait? / demanderai?

Fun fact: In (very) exceptional cases in France, you can marry a deceased person with the permission of the President. (Good God, that sounds very creepy when I say it like that... Maybe I should specify that this is for cases like when your partner dies from a car crash or a long disease.)

Exercise 20.2 - Conjugate "être" (to be), "avoir" (to have) and "aller" (to go) in the present conditional:

	être	avoir	aller
Je			
Tu			
Il/Elle			
Nous			
Vous			
Ils/Elles			

Exercice 20.3 - Choose the correct answer:

1. ____-je avoir un thé, s'il vous plaît ? *(Could I have a glass of tea, please?)*

   a. Pourrait   b. Pourrai   c. Pourrais

2. Il ____ aller au Canada pour ses prochaines vacances. *(He would like to go to Canada for his next vacations.)*

   a. voudrais   b. voudrait   c. voudra

3. Si j'avais soif, je ____ de l'eau. *(If I was thirsty, I'd drink some water.)*

   a. boira   b. boirais   c. boirait

4. Si le ciel était moins nuageux, il ___ les étoiles. *(If the sky was less cloudy, he would see the stars.)*

   a. verrait   b. verrais   c. verra

5. En lisant ce livre, elle ____son français. *(By reading this book, she would improve her French.)*

   a. améliorerait   b. améliorerais   c. améliorera

Exercise 20.4 - For each sentence, say if the conditional is used to ask politely, to say what you would like or need, or to make a suggestion:

1. Pourrais-tu me passer le sel, s'il te plaît? *(Could you pass me the salt please?)*

   _____

2. Je voudrais un peu de silence. *(I would like some silence.)*

   _____

3. Je devrais lui demander. *(I would need to ask her.)*

   _____

4. On pourrait prendre le métro pour y aller ? *(We could take the metro to go there.)*

   _____

5. Voudriez-vous venir avec nous ? *(Would you like to come with us?)*

   _____

Exercise 20.5 - Conjugate the verbs in brackets in the present conditional:

1. Je (aimer) _____ aller à la plage. *(I would like to go to the beach.)*

2. Nous (devoir) _____ partir parce que nous sommes déjà en retard. *(We should leave because we're already late.)*

3. Si vous aimez les haricots, vous en (manger) _____ souvent. *(If you liked beans, you would eat them often.)*

4. Elles (aimer) _____ bien devenir des stars. *(They would like to become stars.)*

5. Je te (croire) _____ si tu me montres une preuve. *(I would believe you if you showed me proof.)*

Exercise 20.6 - Conjugate "manger" (to eat), "partir" (to leave) and "croire" (to believe) in the conditional:

	manger	partir	croire
Je			
Tu			
Il/Elle			
Nous			
Vous			
Ils/Elles			

Exercise 20.7 - For each sentence, say if the conditional is used to nag/complain or to make a suggestion:

1. On pourrait sortir boire un verre, si tu veux ? *(We could go out for a drink if you want.)*

   _____

2. Est-ce que ça te dirait d'aller au cinéma ? *(Would you like to go to the movies?)*

   _____

3. Tu devrais dormir au lieu de regarder la télévision. *(You should sleep instead of watching the television.)*

   _____

4. Si tu m'aidais, nous finirons plus vite. *(If you would help me we will finish faster.)*

   _____

5. Il devrait faire plus attention à sa santé. *(He should pay more attention to his health.)*

   _____

Exercise 20.8 - Conjugate the verbs in brackets in the present conditional:

1. S'il faisait beau, je (aller) _____ me promener. *(If it was sunny, I would go for a walk.)*

2. Si tu faisais attention, tu ne (casser) _____ pas les verres. *(If you were careful, you would not break the glasses.)*

3. Si je gagnais au loto, je (acheter) _____ une voiture. *(If I won the lotto I would buy a car.)*

4. S'ils avaient du temps, ils (venir) _____ me rendre visite en été. *(I they had time, they would come visit me in the summer.)*

5. S'il cessait de pleuvoir, vous (pouvoir) _____ sécher votre linge. *(If it stopped raining, you could dry your clothes.)*

ANSWERS:

Exercise 20.1
Track 56

1/ Si nous avions de l'argent, nous donnerions à la Croix-Rouge. 2/ Nous aimerions vous voir plus souvent. 3/ Si tu m'aidais, je finirais ce travail plus vite. 5/ S'il n'était pas si cher, je commanderais ce manteau. 6/ S'il n'était pas fatigué, je lui demanderais de m'aider.

Exercise 20.2

	être	**avoir**	**aller**
Je	serais	aurais	irais
Tu	serais	aurais	irais
Il/Elle	serait	aurait	irait
Nous	serions	aurions	irions
Vous	seriez	auriez	iriez
Ils/Elles	seraient	auraient	iraient

Exercice 20.3
1/ Pourrais 2/ voudrait 3/ boirais 4/ verrait 5/ améliorerait

Exercise 20.4

1/ To ask politely 2/ To say what you would like 3/ To say what you would need 4/ Make a suggestion 5/ Ask politely

Exercise 20.5

1/ J'aimerais aller à la plage. 2/ Nous devrions partir parce que nous sommes déjà en retard. 3/ Si vous aimez les haricots, vous en mangeriez souvent. 4/Elles aimeraient bien devenir des stars. 5/ Je te croirais si tu me montres une preuve.

Exercise 20.6

	manger	**partir**	**croire**
Je	mangerais	partirais	croirais
Tu	mangerais	partirais	croirais
Il/Elle	mangerait	partirait	croirait
Nous	mangerions	partirions	croirions
Vous	mangeriez	partiriez	croiriez
Ils/Elles	mangeraient	partiraient	croiraient

Exercise 20.7

1/ To make a suggestion. 2/ To make a suggestion. 3/ To nag/complain.
4/ To nag/complain. 5/ To make a suggestion.

Exercise 20.8

1/ S'il faisait beau, j'irais me promener. 2/ Si tu faisais attention, tu ne casserais pas les verres. 3/ Si je gagnais au loto, j'achèterais une voiture. 4/ S'ils avaient du temps, ils viendraient me rendre visite en été. 5/ S'il cessait de pleuvoir, vous pourriez sécher votre linge.

DAY 21
ADVERBS

Adverbs are some of the most hardworking words you'll ever find. They appear together with verbs, adjectives, and other adverbs, and give more information about when, where, how, or to what extent something happens.

Oh, and they pepper your speech too, making it sound more specific and a lot more colourful.

Here are some things you need to remember about adverbs.

HOW TO FORM ADVERBS

- French adverbs NEVER change their form! (Hooray!) But there is one exception to this: the word **"tout"** which can change in some phrases.

- In French, just as in English, the adverbs are formed using the adjectives.

- In the same manner that most English adverbs end in *-ly* (*beautifully, nicely, sweetly*), a lot of adverbs end in *-ment*. This is formed through the feminine singular form of the adjective. The *-ment* ending is added to make it an adverb.

  Examples:

    o **heureuse** becomes **heureusement** (which means *fortunately, luckily or happily*)
    o **douce** becomes **doucement** (meaning *slowly* or *gently*)

- For adjectives that end in **-é**, **-i**, or **u**, the adverb ending to be added is also **-ment**, but the adjective it is added to is the masculine form.

  Example:

    o **vrai** becomes **vraiment** (meaning *truly*).

Note that the feminine form is **"vraie"**, but the masculine form is used instead.

- For adjectives that end in -**ant**, the adverb ending is **-amment**, while adjectives that end in -**ent** use the adverb ending -**emment**.

- Some adjectives can also double as adverbs! These include **bon** (*good*), **mauvais** (*bad*), **droit** (*straight*), and a few others.

WHERE TO PUT ADVERBS IN A SENTENCE

Unlike English, where adverbs can appear all over the place, the French adverbs are somewhat more structured and less unruly. Here are the important things for you to remember.

When modifying a verb:

- When short adverbs are used with verbs, the thing to note is whether there are one or more verb words. If there's only one (such as in the present or imperfect tenses), the adverb comes AFTER the verb.

  Example: **Il pleut toujours.** *(It always rains.)*

- For verbs that consist of more than one word, such as the perfect tense, the adverb comes BETWEEN the two verb words.

  For example: **Elle <u>a</u> trop <u>bu</u>.** *(She has drunk too much.)*

- In some cases regarding adverbs that tell you how or where something is done, it usually comes AFTER the verb, regardless of the number of words in the verb. Alternatively, adverbs stating the specific time or day (**aujourd'hui** – *today*; **demain** – *tomorrow*; **hier** – *yesterday*) can be placed at the beginning or end of the sentence.

- When used with an adjective or another adverb:

  Whenever an adverb modifies an adjective or another adverb, it usually comes BEFORE the word it modifies.

  For example:

  o **Je suis très heureuse !** *(I am very happy!)*
  o **C'est une femme très bien habillée !** *(That's a very well-dressed woman!)*

In Negative statements:

- Adverbs used in negative statements come after the word **"pas"**.

  Example: **Elle ne mange pas bien**. *(She does not eat well.)*

LET'S PRACTICE!

Exercise 21.1 - Transform the adjectives in brackets into adverbs to complete the sentences:

1. (Général) _____, je n'ai pas cours le samedi. *(Generally, I don't have classes on Saturdays.)*

2. J'ai eu beaucoup de travail à terminer (dernier) _____. *(I had a lot of work to complete lately.)*

3. Je me suis approché (doux) _____ pour ne pas faire peur au chiot. *(I approached slowly to not scare the puppy.)*

4. Il a (complet) _____ oublié notre rendez-vous. *(He totally forgot our meeting.)*

5. Le peintre passe son pinceau (lent) _____ pour avoir une ligne droite. *(The painter passes his brush slowly to get a straight line.)*

Exercise 21.2 - Transform the adjectives in brackets into adverbs to complete the sentences:

1. Il faut conduire (prudent) _____. *(You must drive carefully.)*

2. J'attendais les prochaines vacances (impatient) _____. *(I was waiting for the next vacation impatiently.)*

3. Le temps semble avancer (lent) _____ à la fin de journée. *(Time seems to move slowly at the end of the day.)*

4. Elle a (brillant) _____ passé son test de conduite. *(She brilliantly passed her driving test.)*

5. J'ai (clair) _____ mal compris ce que vous m'aviez dit. *(I clearly misunderstood what you have told me.)*

Exercise 21.3 - Complete the sentences with correct form of the adverb " tout ":

1. Elle est venue _____ seule. *(She came all alone.)*

2. Ayant honte de ses actions, il est devenu _____ rouge. *(Ashamed of his actions, he turned all red.)*

3. _____ heureuses d'avoir gagné la compétition, elles s'avancent pour prendre leur prix. *(All happy to have won the competition, they advance to take their prize.)*

4. Attention avec la casserole, elle est _____ remplie d'eau chaude. *(Careful with the pan, it is all filled with hot water.)*

5. Elles se sont faites _____ belles pour le grand bal. *(They were all beautiful for the grand ball.)*

Exercise 21.4 - Place the correct adverb:

1. (Général) _____ , ils passent la journée de Noël chez les parents de sa femme. *(They generally spend Christmas Day at his wife's parents'.)*

2. J'ai lu des choses inquiétantes (dernier) _____ sur cet hôpital.

   (I've read some worrying things recently about that hospital.)

3. Faire revenir (doux) _____ la viande dans une cocotte. *(Gently brown the meat in a pan.)*

4. J'ai (complet) _____ oublié de donner à manger à son chat.

   (I completely forgot to feed her cat.)

5. Le professeur parle (lent) _____ aux étudiants. *(The teacher talks slowly to the students.)*

> **Fun fact:** The word "France" means "land of the Franks". The Franks are Germanic tribes who lived in Northern Europe after the fall of the Roman Empire.

ANSWERS:

Exercise 21.1

1/ Généralement, je n'ai pas cours le samedi. 2/ J'ai eu beaucoup de travail à terminer dernièrement. 3/ Je me suis approché doucement pour ne pas faire peur au chiot. 4/ Il a complètement oublié notre rendez-vous. 5/ Le peintre passe son pinceau lentement pour avoir une ligne droite.

Exercise 21.2

1/ Il faut conduire prudemment. 2/ J'attendais les prochaines vacances impatiemment. 3/ Le temps semble avancer lentement à la fin de journée. 4/ Elle a brillamment passé son test de conduite. 5/ J'ai clairement mal compris ce que vous m'aviez dit.

Exercise 21.3

1. Elle est venue toute seule.
2. Ayant honte de ses actions, il est devenu tout rouge.
3. Toutes heureuses d'avoir gagné la compétition, elles s'avancent pour prendre leur prix.
4. Attention avec la casserole, elle est toute remplie d'eau chaude.
5. Elles se sont faites toutes belles pour le grand bal.

Exercise 21.4
Track 57

1/ Généralement, ils passent la journée de Noël chez les parents de sa femme. 2/ J'ai lu des choses inquiétantes dernièrement sur cet hôpital. 3/ Faire revenir doucement la viande dans une cocotte. 4/ J'ai complètement oublié de donner à manger à son chat. 5/ Le professeur parle lentement aux étudiants.

DAY 22
RELATIVE PRONOUNS

Relative pronouns are also relatively easy. These are the words *who*, *which*, *that*, *whom* and *where*, and we all use these in our daily speech.

Examples:

- o *The house <u>where</u> I grew up in was haunted by ghosts.*
- o *The lady <u>who</u> came over used to be a teacher.*
- o *The sandwich <u>that</u> I ate earlier tasted like cardboard.*

Here's what relative pronouns are used for:

- To properly identify the *person*, *place*, or *thing* being referred to in a relative clause.

- To supply more information about the *person*, *place*, or *thing* being talked about.

- To connect the relative clause to the main clause (as a conjunction).

- To replace the subject, direct object, indirect object, or object of preposition in a relative clause.

French relative pronouns work exactly the same way as their English comrades. These are the words **"qui"**, **"que"**, **"lequel"**, **"auquel"**, **"duquel"**, **"dont"** and **"où"**.

Now, let's take a look at each of these.

1. "qui" and "que"

Qui and **que** can both be used to refer to *persons* or *things*. The main differences are:

- **qui** is used for the subject (or indirect object for persons) and after a preposition (**à**, **de** or **pour**). It could mean *"who"*, *"which"*, or *"that"*.

- **que** is for the direct object and could mean *"who"*, *"whom"*, *"which"*, or *"that"*.

    Examples :

    Track 58

    - o **Les amis que je vois le plus.** *(The friends that I see most)*
    - o **La personne à qui il parle.** *(The person he is speaking to)*

Take note: **qui** and **que** have strictly separate uses and cannot be interchanged.

Exercise 22.1 - Complete the sentences with [qui] or [que]:

1. J'ai trouvé l'objet _____ tu avais caché. *(I found the object that you hid.)*

2. Les vacances _____ j'ai prises m'ont fait du bien. *(The holidays that I took did me good.)*

3. As-tu vu le film _____ a gagné l'Oscar ? *(Have you seen the movie that won the Oscar?)*

4. L'homme à _____ je parlais est allé chercher de la nourriture. *(The man I was talking to went to get food.)*

5. L'animal _____ tu as vu n'était pas un renard. *(The animal you saw was not a fox.)*

2. "lequel"

Lequel is the French counterpart for "*which*"and it is used for indirect objects. It follows the prepositions à, de or **pour** and only used when referring to *things* and never about *people*. Moreover, it has to agree with the noun's gender (masculine or feminine) and number (singular or plural).

- Masculine singular – **lequel**

- Masculine plural – **lesquels**

- Feminine singular – **laquelle**

- Feminine plural – **lesquelles**

    Examples:

    Track 59

    o **le livre pour lequel elle est connue** *(the book she is famous for)*
    o **la table sur laquelle j'ai mis mon sac** *(the table I put my bag on)*

Take note that **lequel** changes into different words when combined with the prepositions à and **de**.

- **à + lequel** becomes **auquel**

- **à + laquelle** is still **à laquelle** (remains the same)

- **à + lesquels** becomes **auxquels**

- **à + lesquelles** becomes **auxquelles**

- **de + lequel** becomes **duquel**

- **de + laquelle** is still **de laquelle** (remains the same)

- **de + lesquels** becomes **desquels**

- **de + lesquelles** becomes **desquelles**

Exercise 22.2 - Complete the sentence with the right form of "lequel":

1. _____ de ces robes est ta préférée ? *(Which one of these dresses is your favourite?)*

2. Entre tous ces bonbons, _____ tu voudrais ? *(Between all these sweets, which ones would you like?)*

3. C'est le seul musée dans _____ on peut trouver ce genre d'expositions. *(This is the only museum where you can find this kind of exhibition.)*

4. Le cours d'informatique _____ j'ai souscrit est un peu compliqué.

   (The computer course I subscribed to is a little complicated.)

5. Elle pose son sac à dos _____ elle sort des feuilles et un stylo. *(She puts down her backpack from which she gets out papers and a pen.)*

Exercise 22.3 - Complete the sentences with "auquel" or "duquel":

1. Le monsieur _____ je me suis adressé est très gentil. *(The gentleman to whom I spoke was very kind.)*

2. C'est le film au milieu _____ je me suis endormi, il était bien ennuyant. *(It's the movie in the middle of which I fell asleep. It was very boring.)*

3. Le tiroir _____ elle a sorti le carnet était plein à ras bord. *(The drawer from which she pulled out the notebook was full to the rim.)*

4. L'homme devant nous est celui _____ j'ai vendu les lunettes. *(The man in front of us is the one to whom I sold the glasses.)*

5. Le chemin au bout _____ se trouve la pharmacie n'est pas très bien éclairé. *(The path at the end of which is the pharmacy is not very well lit.)*

3. "don't"

When translated in English, it means *"whose"*, *"of whom"*, *"of which"*. It may be used to refer to *persons* or *things*. The good news is, it does not change its form, nor does it have to agree with anything!

Some examples :

Track 60

- o **les films dont tu parles** *(the films you are talking about)* – plural
- o **la femme dont la voiture est en panne** *(the woman whose car has broken down)* – singular

4. "où"

This is used for places and times. Its English counterparts could be *"where"*, *"when"* or even *"which"* and *"that"*, depending on how it is used.

Some examples:

Track 61

- o **Paris est la ville où on peut manger les meilleurs escargots.**
  (Paris is the city where we can eat the best snails.)
- o **C'est l'année où ils ont gagné la Coupe du monde.**
  (That's the year they won the World Cup.)
  In addition, **où** can also be used after prepositions.
- o **La ville d'où elle vient...** *(The city where she's from...)*

Exercise 22.4 - Complete the sentences with [dont] or [où]:

1. C'est l'artiste _____ tout le monde parle en ce moment. *(It's the artist everyone is talking about right now.)*

2. Montre-moi les affaires _____ tu voudrais te débarrasser. *(Show me your things that you want to get rid of.)*

3. La ville _____ ils sont allés ne semblait pas très accueillante. *(The city where they went didn't seem very welcoming.)*

4. Ça s'est passé la semaine _____ il est parti en Irlande. *(It happened the week he had gone to Ireland.)*

5. Montre-moi le restaurant _____ tu m'as parlé l'autre jour. *(Show me the restaurant you told me about the other day.)*

LET'S PRACTICE MORE!

Exercise 22.5 - Choose the right pronoun:

1. Le théâtre est quelque chose _____ m'intéresse beaucoup. (*The theatre is something I'm very interested in.*)

    lequel? / que? / dont? / qui?

2. La personne _____ ils parlent est un acteur célèbre. (*The person they're talking about is a famous actor.*)

    qu'? / dont? / qui? / lequel?

3. Nos voisins ont un chien _____ nos enfants ont très peur. (*Our neighbours have a dog our children are very frightened of.*)

    dont? / de qui? / duquel? / que?

4. Je connais quelqu'un _____ peut nous aider. (*I know someone who can help us.*)

    que? / qui? / dont? / lequel?

5. C'est ton cousin _____ j'ai vu à la bibliothèque ? (*Was it your cousin I saw in the library?*)

    laquelle? / qui? / dont? / que?

> **Fun fact:** France is the first manufacturer of wine in the world.

Exercise 22.6 - Complete the sentences with the correct relative pronoun:

1. Je connais quelqu'un _____ peut nous aider. (*I know someone who can help us.*)

2. À _____ as-tu donné la lampe du salon ? (*To whom did you give the living room lamp?*)

3. La série _____ je t'ai parlé est enfin sortie. (*The show I talked to you about is finally out.*)

4. La salle _____ elle a mis ses affaires est fermée à clé. (*The room where she put her belongings is locked.*)

5. Le bâtiment _____ il est sorti était une banque. *(The building he came out of used to be a bank.)*

Exercise 22.7 - Choose the correct answer:

1. La voiture ___ j'ai achetée est rouge. *(The car that I bought is red.)*

   a. qui   b. que   c. laquelle

2. J'ai vu ma cousine aujourd'hui, ___ tu as rencontrée l'autre jour. *(I saw my cousin today, whom you met the other day.)*

   a. qui   b. laquelle   c. lequel

3. La voisine à ___ tu as donné du sucre te remercie. *(The neighbor to whom you gave sugar thanks you.)*

   a. que   b. qui   c. lequel

4. Le jeune homme ___ le chien est malade est parti voir le vétérinaire. *(The young man whose dog is sick has gone to see the vet.)*

   a. qui   b. lequel   c. dont

5. La boulangerie ___ j'ai acheté ce croissant est fermée à cette heure. *(The bakery where I bought this croissant is closed at this time.)*

   a. dont   b. où   c. lequel

ANSWERS:

Exercise 22.1

1/ J'ai trouvé l'objet que tu avais caché. 2/ Les vacances que j'ai prises m'ont fait du bien. 3/ As-tu vu le film qui a gagné l'Oscar ? 4/ L'homme à qui je parlais est allé chercher de la nourriture. 5/ L'animal que tu as vu n'était pas un renard.

Exercise 22.2

1/ Laquelle de ces robes est ta préférée ? 2/ Entre tous ces bonbons, lesquels / lequel (is also acceptable) tu voudrais ? 3/ C'est le seul musée dans lequel on peut trouver ce genre d'expositions. 4/ Le cours d'informatique auquel j'ai souscrit est un peu compliqué. 5/ Elle pose son sac à dos duquel elle sort des feuilles et un stylo.

Exercise 22.3

1/ Le monsieur auquel je me suis adressé est très gentil. 2/ C'est le film au milieu duquel je me suis endormi, il était bien ennuyant. 3/ Le tiroir duquel elle a sorti le carnet était plein à ras bord. 4/ L'homme devant nous est celui auquel j'ai vendu les lunettes. 5/ Le chemin au bout duquel se trouve la pharmacie n'est pas très bien éclairé.

Exercise 22.4

1/ C'est l'artiste dont tout le monde parle en ce moment. 2/ Montre-moi les affaires dont tu voudrais te débarrasser. 3/ La ville où ils sont allés ne semblait pas très accueillante. 4/ Ça s'est passé la semaine où il est parti en Irlande. 5/ Montre-moi le restaurant dont tu m'as parlé l'autre jour.

Exercise 22.5

1/ Le théâtre est quelque chose qui m'intéresse beaucoup. 2/ La personne dont ils parlent est un acteur célèbre. 3/ Nos voisins ont un chien dont nos enfants ont très peur. 4/ Je connais quelqu'un qui peut nous aider. 5/ C'est ton cousin que j'ai vu à la bibliothèque ?

Exercise 22.6

1/ Je connais quelqu'un qui peut nous aider. 2/ À qui as-tu donné la lampe du salon ? 3/ La série dont je t'ai parlé est enfin sortie. 4/ La salle où elle a mis ses affaires est fermée à clé. 5/ Le bâtiment duquel il est sorti était une banque.

Exercise 22.7

1/ Que 2/ Laquelle 3/ Qui 4/ Dont 5/ Où

DAY 23
REFLEXIVE VERBS

The interesting thing about the reflexive verbs (and the one thing that makes them different) is that they use the same subject and object. Reflexive verbs often appear in English together with reflexive pronouns such as *myself, himself, herself, or themselves*. (Example: *The cat cleaned itself.*)

It basically works the same way in French, except that the reflexive verbs are more widely used compared to English.

Here are the important things to remember about French reflexive verbs:

- Reflexive verbs "reflect back" to the subject. (See the concept there?) This means the subject performs the action upon itself.

- A reflexive verb is made up of a reflexive pronoun and a verb.

- These verbs appear in the dictionaries as se + the infinitive form.

  Some examples:

  Track 64

  - **s'adresser à** *(to address, speak to)*
  - **s'approcher de** *(to approach)*
  - **s'amuser** *(to enjoy oneself)*
  - **s'appeler** *(to be called)*
  - **s'asseoir** *(to sit down)*
  - **se baigner** *(to swim)*
  - **se brosser (les cheveux, les dents)** *(to brush (one's hair, one's teeth))*
  - **se casser (la jambe, le bras)** *(to break (one's leg, one's arm))*
  - **se coiffer** *(to fix one's hair)*
  - **se coucher** *(to go to bed)*
  - **se couper** *(to cut oneself)*
  - **se dépêcher** *(to hurry)*
  - **se déshabiller** *(to get undressed)*
  - **se doucher** *(to take a shower)*
  - **s'énerver** *(to get annoyed)*
  - **se laver** *(to wash)*

- Common things about reflexive verbs are: they all have something to do with body parts, personal state, clothing, hygiene, or location.

- Several reflexive verbs also have uses that are non-reflexive. Their meanings may also change slightly according to the usage.

How to form the reflexive verb in the present tense:

- First of all, you have to decide which reflexive pronoun to use. It could be any of the following:

Subject pronoun	Reflexive pronoun	What it means
Je	**me (m')**	*myself*
Tu	**te (t')**	*yourself*
il/ elle/ on	**se (s')**	*himself / herself/ itself/ oneself*
nous	**nous**	*ourselves*
vous	**vous**	*yourself (formal)/ yourselves (formal or informal)*
ils/ elles	**se (s')**	*themselves*

- The basic format looks like this: **subject pronoun + reflexive pronoun + reflexive verb.**

- The present tense form and the endings to be used remain the same: **-e, -es, -e, -ons, -ez,** and **-ent**. (See the lesson on present tense for more information.)

Some examples:

  o **je me lave** *(I wash myself)*
  o **tu me laves** *(you wash yourself)*
  o **il se lave** *(he washes himself)*
  o **nous nous lavons** *(you wash yourselves)*
  o **vous vous lavez** *(we wash ourselves)*
  o **ils se lavent** *(they wash themselves)*

- Please note that nous, vous, and se can mean two or more people and can be used to mean to each other or to one another.

Example: **Les trois filles se ressemblent.** *(The three girls resemble each other.)*

Exercise 23.1 - Conjugate "se laver" (to wash oneself), "s'amuser" (to have fun) and "s'asseoir" (to sit down) in the present tense:

	se laver	s'amuser	s'asseoir
Je			
Tu			
Il/Elle			
Nous			
Vous			
Ils/Elles			

Exercise 23.2 - Conjugate the verbs in brackets in the present tense:

1. Je (se lever) _____ très tôt chaque matin. *(I wake up very early every morning.)*

2. Il (s'installer) _____ à cet hôtel à chaque fois qu'il vient ici. *(He stays at this hotel every time he comes here.)*

3. Nous (se brosser) _____ les dents après chaque repas. *(We brush our teeth after every meal.)*

4. Tu (se laver) _____ les mains combien de fois par jour ? *(How many times do you wash your hands per day?)*

5. Ils (se saluer) _____ très poliment. *(They salute each other very politely.)*

Where to put the reflexive pronoun:

- For present tense uses, the reflexive pronoun always comes BEFORE the verb.

- For negative commands (telling someone not to do something), the reflexive pronoun also comes BEFORE the verb.

- For positive commands, the reflexive pronoun comes AFTER the verb.

LET'S PRACTICE MORE!

Exercise 23.3 - Choose the right connector between:

1. Je (s'asseoir) _____ dans le fauteuil. *(I sat down on the armchair.)*

   m'est assis? / me sont assise? / me suis assis? / me sont asseoir?

2. Est-ce que tu (se brosser) _____ les dents ? *(Have you cleaned your teeth?)*

   t'es brossé? / t'as brossé? / t'est brossé? / te suis brossé?

3. Je (se décider) _____ à vivre en France. *(I've decided to live in France.)*

   m'ai décidé? / me suis décider? / me suis décidé? / me suis décidés?

4. Il (se demander) _____ pourquoi elle était en retard. *(He wondered why she was late.)*

   s'est demandées? / s'est demandée? / s'est demandé? / s'est demandés?

5. Je (se lever) _____ de bonne heure. *(I got up early.)*

   m'ai levé? / me suis levé? / m'est levé? / suis levé?

> ***Fun facts:*** There is a street named after Victor Hugo in every town in France.

Exercise 23.4 - Choose the correct answer:

1. Je ____ pour arriver à temps. *(I hurry to arrive on time.)*

   a. me dépêche   b. me dépêches   c. tu dépêches

2. Vous ____ un gâteau ? *(Are you making yourselves a cake?)*

   a. vous faites   b. nous faites   c. vous faisons

3. Il ___ souvent dans ce parc. *(He often walks in this park.)*

   a. te promène   b. se promène   c. se promener

4. Les enfants ____ pour faire peur à leur père. *(The kids hide to scare their father.)*

    a. se cache   b. se cachent   c. nous cachent

5. Vous ____ de la chanson de Julien ? *(Do you remember Julien's song?)*

    a. se souvenez   b. vous souvenir   c. vous souvenez

Exercise 23.5 - Transform these sentences into the negative form:

1. Il se souvient de son enfance. *(He remembers his childhood.)*

    _____

2. Je me brosse les dents après chaque repas. *(I brush my teeth after each meal.)*

    _____

3. On s'appelle tous les jours. *(We call each other every day.)*

    _____

4. Je me couche tard le soir. *(I sleep late at night.)*

    _____

5. Je m'énerve facilement. *(I get angry very easily.)*

    _____

Exercise 23.6: Conjugate the verbs in brackets in the present tense:

1. On (s'amuser) _____ beaucoup ici. *(We're having a lot of fun here.)*

2. Il (s'approcher) _____ de moi et me dit " je t'aime ". *(He gets closer and tells me "I love you".)*

3. Je (se couper) _____ le doigt en préparant la salade. *(I cut my finger while preparing the salad.)*

4. Elle (se casser) _____ la jambe en tombant dans l'escalier. *(She broke her leg while falling down the stairs.)*

5. Je (se déshabiller) _____ avant de prendre une douche. *(I get undressed before taking a shower.)*

ANSWERS:

Exercise 23.1

	se laver	s'amuser	s'asseoir
Je	me lave	m'amuse	m'assois
Tu	te laves	t'amuses	t'assois
Il/Elle	se lave	s'amuse	s'assoit
Nous	nous lavons	nous amusons	nous assoyons
Vous	vous lavez	vous amusez	vous assoyez
Ils/Elles	se lavent	s'amusent	s'assoient

Exercise 23.2

1/ Je me lève très tôt chaque matin. 2/ Il s'installe à cet hôtel à chaque fois qu'il vient ici. 3/ Nous nous brossons les dents après chaque repas. 4/ Tu te laves les mains combien de fois par jour ? 5/ Ils se saluent très poliment.

Exercise 23.3

1/ Je me suis assis dans le fauteuil. 2/ Est-ce que tu t'es brossé les dents ? 3/ Je me suis décidé à vivre en France. 4/ Il s'est demandé pourquoi elle était en retard. 5/ Je me suis levé de bonne heure.

Exercise 23.4

1/ me dépêche 2/ vous faites 3/ se promène 4/ se cachent 5/ vous souvenez

Exercise 23.5

1/ Il ne se souvient pas de son enfance. 2/ Je ne me brosse pas les dents après chaque repas. 3/ On ne s'appelle pas tous les jours. 4/ Je ne me couche pas tard le soir. 5/ Je ne m'énerve pas facilement.

Exercise 23.6

1/ On s'amuse beaucoup ici. 2/ Il s'approche de moi et me dit " je t'aime ". 3/ Je me coupe le doigt en préparant la salade. 4/ Elle se casse la jambe en tombant dans l'escalier. 5/ Je me déshabille avant de prendre une douche.

DAY 24
TIME, DURATION, AND RELATED EXPRESSIONS

There is huge volume of vocabulary and expressions pertaining to time, but this lesson aims to narrow it down to the most important parts. Below are the words, phrases, and expressions that you should remember when it comes to stating time in French.

USEFUL WORDS AND PHRASES

- **How often? (frequency)**

Track 66

- **une fois** - *once*
- **une fois par semaine** - *once a week*
- **deux fois par semaine** - *twice a week*
- **quotidien** - *daily*
- **tous les jours** - *every day*
- **tous les deux jours** - *every other day*
- **hebdomadaire** - *weekly*
- **toutes les semaines** - *every week*
- **mensuel** - *monthly*
- **annuel** – *yearly*

- **When did/will it happen? (relative time)**

Track 67

- **avant-hier** - *the day before yesterday*
- **hier** - *yesterday*
- **aujourd'hui** - *today*
- **maintenant** - *now*
- **demain** - *tomorrow*
- **après-demain** - *the day after tomorrow*
- **la veille** - *the day before*
- **le lendemain** - *the day after, the next day*
- **la semaine passée/dernière** - *last week*
- **la dernière semaine**- *the final week*
- **la semaine prochaine**- *next week*

- **il y a peu de temps** - *a little while ago*

- **Points in time / periods of time**

Track 68

- **une seconde** - *second*
- **une minute** - *minute*
- **une heure** - *hour*
- **un jour, une journée** - *day*
- **une semaine** - *week*
- **un mois** - *month*
- **un an, une année** - *year*
- **une décennie** - *decade*
- **un siècle** - *century*
- **un millénaire** - *millenium*
- **le matin** - *morning*
- **l'après-midi** - *afternoon*
- **midi** - *noon*
- **le soir** - *evening*
- **le crépuscule** – *dusk*
- **l'aube** – *dawn*
- **la nuit** - *night*
- **minuit** - *midnight*

Exercise 24.1: Choose the correct answer:

1. ____, j'irai en vacances. (____, *I will go on vacation.*)

   a. La semaine dernière   b. La semaine prochaine   c. Hier

2. Il a pris le train pour Londres ___ (*He took the train to London ___.*)

   a. hier   b. demain   c. le lendemain

3. Nous avons un grand match ___. (*We have a big match ___.*)

   a. la semaine prochaine   b. la semaine passée   c. la dernière semaine

4. Elle te rendra visite ___. (*She will visit you ___.*)

   a. avant-hier   b. après-demain   c. la semaine dernière

5. Il le fera ___. (*He will do it ___.*)

   a. hier   b. dans une minute   c. maintenant

Exercise 24.2 - Translate the words from English to French:

1. A day   - _____

2. A week   - _____

3. A month - _____

4. A year   - _____

5. Once   - _____

- **Prepositions about time**

  - à – Used when expressing the time when a certain action will occur.

    Example: **À 8 heures.** *(At 8 o'clock.)*

  - **en** – Used when expressing the length of time, season, month, or year. Example: **En été.** *(In summer.)*

  - **dans** – Used when telling the amount of time before an action will happen. Example: **Nous mangerons dans 10 minutes.** *(We'll eat in 10 minutes.)*

  - **depuis** – Used when saying the duration of an ongoing activity.

    Example: **Nous parlons depuis une heure**. *(We've been talking for an hour.)*

  - **pendant/durant** – Refers to the entire duration of an action.

    Example: **Il a dormi pendant/durant 12 heures.** *(He slept for 12 hours.)*

  - **pour** – Refers to the duration of a future event.

    Example: Il va parler pour une heure. *(He's going to speak for an hour.)*

Exercise 24.3 - Complete the sentences with [à], [en] or [dans]:

1. Je me réveille _____ 8 heures tous les matins. *(I wake up at 8 o'clock every morning.)*

2. Elle a fini son travail _____ l'aube. *(She finished her work at dawn.)*

3. _____ hiver, les arbres perdent leur feuillage. *(In winter, trees lose their foliage.)*

4. Je terminerai ma formation _____ une semaine. *(I will finish my training in a week.)*

5. Je serai là-bas _____ une minute. *(I'll be there in a minute.)*

Exercise 24.4 - Complete the sentences with [depuis], [pendant], or [pour]:

1. Je l'attends ici _____ une heure. (*I have been waiting for him here for an hour.*)

2. Il peut retenir sa respiration sous l'eau _____ trois minutes. (*He can hold his breath under water for three minutes.*)

3. Il a voyagé _____ un mois. (*He traveled for a month*)

4. J'ai encore du travail _____ deux heures. (*I still have to work for two hours.*)

5. Elle attend une réponse _____ hier. (*She's been waiting for an answer since yesterday.*)

LET'S PRACTICE MORE!

Exercise: 24.5 - Choose the right answer:

1. Je préfère voyager _____ été.

   a) dans   b) en

2. Elle va partir pour l'université _____ deux mois.

   a) dans   b) en

3. Je dois m'en aller _____ quelques minutes.

   a) dans   b) en

4. Je vais commencer mes devoirs _____ dix minutes.

   a) dans   b) en

5. Il s'est rasé _____ deux minutes.

   a) dans   b) en

> ***Fun fact:*** April Fool's Day is believed to have originated in France, in 1564, when the country started following the Gregorian Calendar. Those that did not know about the change in the calendar were mocked as they continued to believe that the 1st of April was the first day of the French new year.

Exercise 24.6 - Complete the sentences with the correct preposition:

1. _____ été, il fait très chaud. *(In summer, it's very hot.)*

2. Je vis ici _____ une année. *(I've been living here for a year.)*

3. _____ minuit, toutes les lumières sont éteintes. *(At midnight, all lights are off.)*

4. Votre repas sera prêt _____ dix minutes. *(Your meal will be ready in ten minutes.)*

5. J'ai joué au football _____ des années. *(I played football for years.)*

ANSWERS:

Exercise 24.1

1/ La semaine prochaine 2/ hier 3/ la semaine prochaine 4/ après-demain 5/ dans une minute

Exercise 24.2

1/ Un jour/Une journée 2/ Une semaine 3/ Un mois 4/ Une année 5/ Une fois

Exercise 24.3

1/ Je me réveille à 8 heures tous les matins. 2/ Elle a fini son travail à l'aube. 3/ En hiver, les arbres perdent leur feuillage. 4/ Je terminerai ma formation dans une semaine. 5/ Je serai là-bas dans une minute.

Exercise 24.4

1/ Je l'attends ici depuis une heure. 2/ Il peut retenir sa respiration sous l'eau pour trois minutes. 3/ Il a voyagé pendant un mois. 4/ J'ai encore du travail pour deux heures. 5/ Elle attend une réponse depuis hier.

Exercise: 24.5
Track 69

1/ Je préfère voyager en été. 2/ Elle va partir pour l'université dans deux mois. 3/ Je dois m'en aller dans quelques minutes. 4/ Je vais commencer mes devoirs dans dix minutes. 5/ Il s'est rasé en deux minutes.

Exercise 24.6

1/ En été, il fait très chaud. 2/ Je vis ici depuis une année. 3/ À minuit, toutes les lumières sont éteintes. 4/ Votre repas sera prêt dans dix minutes. 5/ J'ai joué au football pendant/durant des années.

DAY 25
STRESSED PRONOUNS

In the previous lessons, we talked about several kinds of pronouns. Guess what? There's yet another type of pronoun I would like to introduce to you:

STRESSED PRONOUNS!!! *(Ta-daaah!)*

What are these and what do they do?

Will it make you "stressed" out? No.

Are these pronouns "stressed" and "overworked"? Um, no.

Here's what they are:

- They come after prepositions such as **"avec"** (*with*), **"pour"** (*for*), **"sans"** (*without*), **"chez"** (*at the house of*), and so on. BUT —

- They could also appear after **"c'est"**, or even alone!

In short, they are very flexible, have so many uses, and can be used anywhere in a sentence. (Cooool.)

Here are the different stressed pronouns:	
1. **moi** – *me*	5. **nous** – *us*
2. **toi** – *you* [singular informal]	6. **vous** – *you* [singular formal or plural formal and informal]
3. **lui** – *him*	7. **eux** – *them* [masculine]
4. **elle** – *her*	8. **elles** – *them* [feminine]

Some examples:

Track 70

- ○ **Elle a peur de lui**. *(She is scared of him.)*
- ○ **Je pense à toi**. *(I'm thinking of you.)*
- ○ **Il va avec eux**. *(He goes with them.)*

Here are the other uses of stressed pronouns:

- **To emphasize pronouns.** There's this thing called **"accent tonique"** (*tonic accent*) in French which emphasizes words. In English, you normally just say the word more loudly or slowly, but in French, this won't do. In cases such as these, stressed pronouns are used. This kind of speech will be more effective at drawing attention to the pronoun.

Example: **Je ne sais pas, moi.**

This is kind of like saying *"I don't know"* but with considerably more feeling and emphasis on the *I.*

In a similar manner, it also appears after **c'est** or **ce sont** - also with the purpose of emphasizing the pronoun.

- **To point out a second subject or object in a sentence.** When there is more than one subject or object, the stressed pronoun comes to the rescue.

Example: **Je les ai vus, lui et elle.** *(I saw him and her.)*

- **To ask and answer questions.** When asking questions like, *"Who wants to go?"* This could be answered simply with a stressed pronoun. In the same way, you could also ask questions by using these pronouns, such as **et toi?** *(and you?)*

- **To take the place of indirect object pronouns in some cases where they cannot be used.** Some verbs just don't like indirect object pronouns, so you use a stressed pronoun instead.

Example: **Je pense à toi.** *(I'm thinking of you.)*

LET'S PRACTICE!

Exercise 25.1 - Choose the right answer:

1. Elle a écrit l'histoire _____-même. *(She wrote the story __ herself.)*

   a) elle   b) lui   c) soi

2. _____ aussi, il est fatigué. *(__ also, he is tired.)*

   a) Il   b) Lui   c) Soi

3. J'espère que tu l'achèteras pour _____. *(Hope you buy it for __.)*

   a) je   b) moi   c) me

4. _____, tu es intelligent. *(__, you are smart.)*

   a) Tu   b) Toi

5. C'est _____ (Jean) qui a dit la verité. *(It was __ (John) who told the truth.)*

   a) il   b) lui

Fun fact: Another interesting French fact is that a number of words in the English Language are derived from the names of prominent French individuals. For example, the word 'chauvinism' is believed to have originated from Nicola Chauvin, a soldier in Napolean's army whose loyalty to the emperor was legendary. The word 'sadism' originated from Marquis de Sade, a French nobleman who led the life of a libertine and wrote sadistic novels.

Exercise 25.2 - Choose the correct answer:

1. ____ aussi, elle travaille ici. *(She works here, too.)*

   a. Elle   b. Il   c. Lui

2. ___ tu me comprends. *(You understand me.)*

   a. Toi   b. Lui   c. Moi

3. Pendant que ___ il jouait, sa sœur faisait ses devoirs. *(While he was playing, his sister did her homework.)*

    a. moi   b. lui   c. elle

4. Contrairement à toi, je lui fais confiance, ___. *(Unlike you, I trust her.)*

    a. toi   b. moi   c. nous

5. Il va essayer de nous vendre de la contrefaçon, à ___. *(He's going to try to sell a forgery to us.)*

    a. lui   b. nous   c. eux

Exercise 25.3 - Complete the sentences with [moi], [toi], [lui] or [elle]:

1. Chaque fois qu'il nous rend visite, elle se cache. Elle a peur de_____. *(Every time he visits us, she hides. She's afraid of him.)*

2. Elle ne m'a pas menti, _____. *(She didn't lie to me.)*

3. À _____, il m'a dit qu'il voulait une nouvelle voiture. *(He told me that he wanted a new car.)*

4. On pourrait aller chez _____. *(We could go to your place.)*

5. Il veut y aller sans _____. *(He wants to go without her.)*

Exercise 25.4 - Complete the sentences with [avec], [pour], [sans] or [chez]:

1. Tu as oublié tes clés _____ moi. *(You forgot your keys at my place.)*

2. J'ai acheté ce cadeau _____ elle. *(I bought this gift for her.)*

3. Je ne parle plus à Marc. J'ai eu des problèmes _____ lui. *(I don't talk to Marc anymore. I had problems with him.)*

4. Ils ont oublié de m'appeler et sont partis _____ moi. *(They forgot to call me and went without me.)*

5. Ne sois pas timide, viens chanter _____ nous. *(Don't be shy, come sing with us.)*

Exercise 25.5 - Complete the sentences with [nous], [vous], [eux] or [elles]:

1. Venez avec _____ Nous allons au cinéma. *(Come with us. We're going to the cinema.)*

2. Elles sont très énergiques. J'ai essayé de continuer la course avec _____, mais je n'ai pas pu. *(They are very energetic. I tried to continue the race with them, but I could not.)*

3. J'ai apporté ces beignets pour _____. *(I brought these donuts for you.)*

4. _____, ils sont déjà montés sur la montagne. *(They have already climbed the mountain.)*

5. Mais vous avez une plus grande télévision chez _____. *(But you have a bigger television.)*

Exercise 25.6 - Complete the sentences with the correct stressed pronoun. :

1. Il est parti ce matin. Je n'arrête pas de penser à _____. *(He left this morning. I can't stop thinking about him.)*

2. C'est _____ qui m'a aidé avec mon travail. *(It's him who helped me with my work.)*

3. Il a réparé sa voiture _____ -même. *(He repaired his car himself.)*

4. Etienne et Sandra sont déjà assis, mets-toi entre _____. *(Etienne and Sandra are already seated, sit down between them.)*

5. Je crois qu'il faut aller le voir. Et _____, t'en penses quoi ? *(I think we have to go see him. And what do you think?)*

ANSWERS:

Exercise 25.1
Track 71

1/ Elle a écrit l'histoire elle-même. 2/ Lui aussi, il est fatigué. 3/ J'espère que tu l'achèteras pour moi. 4/ Toi, tu es intelligent. 5/ C'est lui (Jean) qui a dit la verité.

Exercise 25.2

1/ Elle 2/ Toi 3/ lui 4/ moi 5/ nous

Exercise 25.3

1/ Chaque fois qu'il nous rend visite, elle se cache. Elle a peur de lui. 2/ Elle ne m'a pas menti, elle. 3/ À moi, il m'a dit qu'il voulait une nouvelle voiture. 4/ On pourrait aller chez toi/vous. 5/ Il veut y aller sans elle.

Exercise 25.4

1/ Tu as oublié tes clés chez moi. 2/ J'ai acheté ce cadeau pour elle. 3/ Je ne parle plus à Marc. J'ai eu des problèmes avec lui. 4/ Ils ont oublié de m'appeler et sont partis sans moi. 5/ Ne sois pas timide, viens chanter avec nous.

Exercise 25.5

1/ Venez avec nous. Nous allons au cinéma. 2/ Elles sont très énergiques. J'ai essayé de continuer la course avec elles, mais je n'ai pas pu. 3/ J'ai apporté ces beignets pour toi/vous. 4/ Eux, ils sont déjà montés sur la montagne. 5/ Mais vous avez une plus grande télévision chez vous.

Exercise 25.6

1/ Il est parti ce matin. Je n'arrête pas de penser à lui. 2/ C'est lui qui m'a aidé avec mon travail. 3/ Il a réparé sa voiture lui-même. 4/ Etienne et Sandra sont déjà assis, mets-toi entre eux. 5/ Je crois qu'il faut aller le voir. Et toi, t'en penses quoi ?

DAY 26
DEMONSTRATIVE PRONOUNS

We already know much about pronouns and their function to replace a noun. In English, the following demonstrative pronouns are also used for this purpose: *this*, *these*, *that*, and *those*.

French demonstrative pronouns work the same way, but with the usual twist - they have to agree with the nouns they're replacing.

Here are the different demonstrative pronouns and the basic rules.

1. "ce"

- **Ce** goes together with the verb **être** which means to be.

  Some examples:

  - **c'est** *(it's or that's)*
  - **c'était** *(it was, that was)*
  - **ce sont** *(it's, that's)*
  - **c'est moi !** *(It's me!)*
  - **c'était mon frère.** *(That was my brother.)*
  - **ce sont eux.** *(That's them.)*

- **Ce** becomes **c'** when it comes before a verb that begins with either **e** or **é**.

- **Ce** is used in the following 3 instances:

  1. To identify a *person* or *thing*, either in a statement or with a question word.

     Example: **Qui est-ce?** *(Who is it?)*, **Ce sont eux.** *(That's them.)*

  2. To go with an adjective that refers to an idea or statement that cannot be classified as masculine or feminine.

     Example: **C'est dangereux !** *(That's dangerous!)*

  3. To put an emphasis on the statement.

     Example: **Ce sont les enfants qui ont fait le gâteau.** *(It was the children who made the cake.)*

Exercise 26.1 - Complete the sentences with [c'est], [c'était] or [ce sont]:

1. J'ai adoré la fête d'hier soir. _____ amusant. *(I loved yesterday's party. It was fun.)*

2. Hier, j'ai dansé pendant toute la soirée. _____ fantastique ! *(Yesterday, I danced all night long. It was fantastic!)*

3. _____ eux qui ont fait tout le travail. *(They are the ones who did all the work.)*

4. Regarde par la fenêtre ! _____ magnifique ! *(Look out the window! It's beautiful!)*

5. _____ fou comment le temps passe vite ! *(It's crazy how time flies.)*

2. "cela", "ça" and "ceci"

- **Cela** and **ça** both mean *"it"*, *"this"*, or *"that"*, and could refer to either a statement, an idea, or an object. The difference between the two is that ça is the less formal one and often appears in everyday speech.

    Examples:

    Track 72

    - **Cela dépend.** *(It depends.)*
    - **Ça ne fait rien.** *(It doesn't matter.)*
- **Ceci** is not as commonly used as **cela** and ça. Its uses are to refer to something that hasn't been previously mentioned, or to show someone a certain thing.

    Examples:

    Track 73

    - **Lisez ceci.** *(Read this.)*
    - **Prends ceci.** *(Take this.)*

Exercise 26.2 - Complete the sentences with [ça] [c'est] or [ceci]:

1. La musique, j'adore _____. *(Music, I love that.)*

2. _____ est mon album photo. *(This is my photo album.)*

3. _____ très gentil de ta part de m'accompagner chez moi. *(It's very nice of you to accompany me to my home.)*

3. "celui", "celle", "ceux" and "celles"

Celui means *"the one"*, and the different forms you use when referring to its feminine and plural forms are below.

- **celui** - masculine singular
- **celle** - feminine singular
- **ceux** - masculine plural
- **celles** - feminine plural

Celui and its different forms are used in the following cases:

- Before **qui**, **que**, or **dont**.

   Example: **Celui dont je t'ai parlé.** *(The one I told you about.)*

- Before prepositions like à, dans, etc.

   Example: **Celui proche de la porte**. *(The one near the door.)*

- With **de** to show that it belongs to someone.

- With the endings **-ci** and **-là** to indicate how far something is from you. Like the demonstrative adjectives, **-ci** is added to mean it is closer, **-là** if it is farther.

   Example: ***Celui-ci ou celui-là ?*** *(This one or that one?)*

Exercise 26.3 - Complete the sentences with [celui], [celle], [ceux], [celles]:

1. Ces deux livres m'appartiennent. _____-là sont à rendre à la bibliothèque. *(These two books are mine. Those are to be returned to the library.)*

2. Tu vois les deux filles là-bas ? _____ qui est à droite est ma sœur. *(You see the two girls there? The right one is my sister.)*

3. Ces gâteaux-là sont bons, mais _____ -ci ne le sont pas. *(These cakes are tasty, but these are not.)*

LET'S PRACTICE!

Exercise 26.4 - Choose the right answer:

1. J'ai trouvé ce livre-ci plus intéressant que _____-là. (*I found this book more interesting than that one.*)
   celui? / ceux? / celles ? / celle?

2. Je n'aime pas cette jupe-là. Je préfère _____-ci. (*I don't like that skirt. I prefer this one.*)
   celles? / celle? / celui? / ceux?

3. Jean m'a montré sa voiture, _____ qu'il vient d'acheter. (*Jean showed me his car, the one he's just bought.*)
   celles? / celui? / ceux? / celle?

4. Cette voiture-ci est française et _____-là est anglaise. (*This car is French and that one is English.*)
   ceux? / celle? / celles? / celui?

5. Est-ce que tu préfères ces chocolats-ci ou _____-là ? (*Do you prefer these chocolates or those chocolates?*)
   ceux? / celles? / celui? / celle ?

> **Fun fact:** France is home to the Louvre, the largest art museum in the world.

Exercise 26.5 - Choose the correct answer:

1. Aujourd'hui, ___est mon anniversaire. (*Today is my birthday.*)

   a. ç›   b. c'   c. celui

2. Arrête de rigoler. Je ne trouve pas ___ amusant. (*Stop laughing. I don't find this funny.*)

   a. ça   b. c'   c. celui

3. ___ qui n'a jamais manqué d'argent, ne peut comprendre. (*The one who never ran out of money can't understand.*)

   a. c'est   b. ça   c. celui

Exercise 26.6 - Complete the sentences with the correct demonstrative pronouns:

1. Cette voiture n'est pas ____ de ma mère. *(This is not my mom's car.)*

2. J'aime ce film, mais je préfère ____ qu'on a vu la dernière fois. *(I like this movie, but I prefer the one we saw last time.)*

3. Il fait froid aujourd'hui. ____ serait mieux de sortir demain. *(It's cold today. It would be better to go out tomorrow.)*

ANSWERS:

Exercise 26.1

1/ J'ai adoré la fête d'hier soir. C'était amusant. 2/ Hier, j'ai dansé pendant toute la soirée. C'était fantastique ! 3/ Ce sont eux qui ont fait tout le travail. 4/ Regarde par la fenêtre ! C'est magnifique ! 5/ C'est fou comment le temps passe vite !

Exercise 26.2

1/ La musique, j'adore ça. 2/ Ceci est mon album photo. 3/ C'est très gentil de ta part de m'accompagner chez moi.

Exercise 26.3

1/ Ces deux livres m'appartiennent. Ceux-là sont à rendre à la bibliothèque. 2/ Tu vois les deux filles là-bas ? Celle qui est à droite est ma sœur. 3/ Ces gâteaux-là sont bons, mais ceux-ci ne le sont pas.

Exercise 26.4

Track 74

1/ J'ai trouvé ce livre-ci plus intéressant que celui-là. 2/ Je n'aime pas cette jupe-là. Je préfère celle-ci. 3/ Jean m'a montré sa voiture, celle qu'il vient d'acheter. 4/ Cette voiture-ci est française et celle-là est anglaise. 5/ Est-ce que tu préfères ces chocolats-ci ou ceux-là ?

Exercise 26.5

1/ Aujourd'hui, c'est mon anniversaire. 2/ Arrête de rigoler. Je ne trouve pas ça amusant. 3/ Celui qui n'a jamais manqué d'argent, ne peut comprendre.

Exercise 26.6

1/ Cette voiture n'est pas celle de ma mère. 2/ J'aime ce film, mais je préfère celui qu'on a vu la dernière fois. 3/ Il fait froid aujourd'hui. Ce/Ça serait mieux de sortir demain.

DAY 27
NUMBERS

Contrary to what you might think, French numbers are actually easy. Well, not too easy when you compare them with the English ones, but at least they look the same, right?

A quick refresher: cardinal numbers are used to tell us how many are there, or the quantity. The other kind of numbers – ordinal – tell us the position or the order in relation to other numbers (e.g., 1st, 2nd, 3rd, 4th, and so on.)

Now, first things first. Here are the numbers in French.

Track 75

1	**un**	ung
2	**deux**	deu
3	**trois**	trwa
4	**quatre**	katr
5	**cinq**	sank
6	**six**	sees or see
7	**sept**	set
8	**huit**	wheat
9	**neuf**	neuf
10	**dix**	deece or dee
11	**onze**	ohn
12	**douze**	dooz
13	**treize**	trayz
14	**quatorze**	kat-ORZ
15	**quinze**	cans
16	**seize**	sayz
17	**dix-sept**	dee-SET
18	**dix-huit**	dee-ZWEET
19	**dix-neuf**	dee-ZNEUF
20	**vingt**	vang

21	**vingt et un**	vang-tay-UNG
22	**vingt-deux**	vang-DEU
23	**vingt-trois**	vang-TRWA
30	**trente**	trongt
40	**quarante**	kar-AHNGT
50	**cinquante**	sank-AHNGT
60	**soixante**	swah-SAHNGT
70	**soixante-dix**	swah-shangt-DEE
80	**quatre-vingt**	katr-VANG
90	**quatre-vingt-dix**	katr-vang-DEE
100	**cent**	sahng
1,000	**mille**	meel
10,000	**dix mille**	dee meel
1,000,000	**un million**	ung mee-LYOHNG

The basic rules:

- From *seventy* to *ninety*, you have to do a tiny bit of addition and multiplication. *Seventy* is **soixante-dix** (60 and 10), *eighty* is **quatre-vingt** (four twenties or 4x20), and *ninety* is **quatre-vingt-dix** (literally, four-twenty-ten).

Examples:

  - *seventy-two* is **soixante-douze** (sixty-twelve)
  - *seventy-nine* is **soixante-dix-neuf** (sixty-ten-nine)
  - *eighty-two* is **quatre-vingt-deux** (four-twenty-two)
  - *ninety-two* is **quatre-vingt-douze** (four-twenty-twelve)

- You use **"et"** for the following numbers:

  - **21 vingt et un**
  - **31 trente et un**
  - **41 quarante et un**
  - **51 cinquante et un**
  - **61 soixante et un**
  - **71 soixante et onze**

- You use *hyphens* when writing the following numbers as words: 17, 18, 19, 22 – 29, 32 – 39 up to 79, and then 80 – 99

- In most instances, cardinal numbers are spelt out. Except for the following:
  - In dates
    Example: **le 29 janvier 1950**
  - In prices
    Example: **L'armoire coûte 449 euros.** *(The cupboard costs 449 euros.)*
  - In weights and measures
    Example: **Vous pesez 56 kilos pour 1,70 mètre.** (*You weigh 56 kilos for 1.70 meters tall.)*
  - In mathematical usage
  - In percentage
  - In addresses and telephone numbers

- To say approximate numbers in French, we add -**aine** to the number. This is equivalent to saying "*about*" or "*around*" in English.

  Examples: **une dizaine** *(about ten)*, **une quinzaine** *(about fifteen).*

- To form ordinal numbers, simply use the cardinal number, drop the last letter **e** (if any), and add the suffix -**ième**. The only exception to this is *premier* (or *première* for feminine) which means first.

  Example: **quatre** becomes **quatrième** and **six** becomes **sixième**.

LET'S PRACTICE!

Exercise 27.1 - Choose the right answer:

1. 7th _____ *(seventh)*

   setième? / septièmme? / septieme? / septième?

2. 500 _____ *(five hundred)*

   cinq-cent? / cinq-cents? / cinq cents? / cinq cent?

3. 8 _____ *(eight)*

   huis? / huite? / hui? / huit?

4. 21 _____ *(twenty-one)*

   vingt un? / vingt et un? / vingt-un? / vingt-et-un?

5. 92 _____ *(ninety-two)*

   quatre-vingt douze? / quatre-vingts-douze? / quatre vingt-douze? / quatre-vingt-douze?

6. Sophie a (5) _____ ans. *(Sophie is five years old.)*

   deux? / cinq? / trois? / quatre?

7. Le bébé a (1) ___ an. *(The baby's one year old.)*

   quatre? / deux? / trois? / un?

8. 570 _____ *(five hundred and seventy)*

   cinq cents soixante-dix? / cinq cent soixante-dix? / cinq-cent soixante-dix? / cinq-cents soixantedix?

> *Fun fact:* From the French Alps to the marvelous beaches lining the azure waters in the French Riviera, France is one of the most visited countries in the world. In 2007, it attracted as many as 81.9 million tourists. This number was greater than its population!

Exercise 27.2 - Choose the correct answer:

1. Marie a (5) _____ ans. *(Marie is 5 years old.)*

   a. cinq   b. six   c. cinquante

2. Il y'a (11) ___ joueurs dans l'équipe. *(There are 11 players on the team.)*

   a. dix-un   b. onze   c. un et un

3. J'ai fini par utiliser (61) _____ planches pour le parquet. *(I ended up using 61 boards for the floor.)*

   a. soixante et un   b. soixante et onze   c. six et un

4. Il est né en ('93) _____. *(He was born in '93.)*

   a. neuvente-trois   b. quatre-vingt-trois   c. quatre-vingt-treize

5. Les réparations ont coûté (400) _____ euros. *(The repairs cost 400 euros.)*

   a. quatre-cent   b. cent   c. quarante-dix

Exercise 27.3 - Translate these numbers from English to French:

1. Twelve   - _____

2. Twenty-two   - _____

3. Thirty-one   - _____

4. Forty-five   - _____

5. Fifty   - _____

Exercise 27.4 - Complete the sentences with the correct ordinal numbers:

1. Je suis la (1st) _____ de ma classe. *(I am the first in my class.)*

2. Barack Obama est le (44th) _____ président des États-Unis. *(Barack Obama is the forty-forth president of the United States.)*

3. C'est la (3rd) _____ fois que je perds aux échecs contre mon père. *(It's the third time I have lost in chess against my father.)*

4. C'est son (13th) _____ mois sans cigarettes. *(It's his thirteenth month without cigarettes.)*

5. J'ai assisté au (72th) _____ anniversaire de ma grand-mère. *(I attended my grandma's seventy-second birthday.)*

Exercise 27.5 - Translate these numbers from English to French:

1. Seventy-two - _____
2. Eighty-five - _____
3. Sixty-three - _____
4. Ninety-four - _____
5. One hundred - _____

Exercise 27.6 - Complete the sentences with the correct approximate numbers:

1. La prof a (about thirty) _____ de copies d'examen à corriger. (*The teacher has about thirty exam copies to check.*)

2. Nos poules ont pondu (about twelve) _____ d'œufs. (*Our chickens laid about twelve eggs.*)

3. Il y avait (about fifty) _____ de feux d'artifice pendant le spectacle. (*There were about fifty fireworks during the show.*)

4. (about a hundred) _____ de personnes sont venues voir son film. (*About a hundred people came to see her movie.*)

5. Je serai chez toi dans (about fifteen) _____ de minutes. (*I'll be at your house in about fifteen minutes.*)

ANSWERS:

Exercise: 27.1
Track 76

1/ septième 2/ cinq cents 3/ huit 4/ vingt et un 5/ quatre-vingt-douze 6/ Sophie a cinq ans. 7/ Le bébé a un an. 8/ cinq cent soixante-dix

Exercise 27.2

1/ cinq 2/ onze 3/ soixante et une 4/ quatre-vingt-treize 5/ quatre-cent

Exercise 27.3

1/ douze 2/ vingt-deux 3/ trente et un 4/ quarante-cinq 5/ cinquante

Exercise 27.4

1/ Je suis la première de ma classe. 2/ Barack Obama est le quarante-quatrième président des États-Unis. 3/ C'est la troisième fois que je perds aux échecs contre mon père. 4/ C'est son treizième mois sans cigarettes. 5/ J'ai assisté au soixante-douzième anniversaire de ma grand-mère.

Exercise 27.5

1/ Soixante-douze 2/ Quatre-vingt-cinq 3/ Soixante-trois 4/ Quatre-vingt-quatorze 5/ Cent

Exercise 27.6

1/ La prof a une trentaine de copies à corriger. 2/ Nos poules ont pondu une douzaine d'œufs. 3/ Il y avait une cinquantaine de feux d'artifice pendant le spectacle. 4/ Une centaine de personnes sont venues voir son film. 5/ Je serai chez toi dans une quinzaine de minutes.

DAY 28
THE PRESENT PARTICIPLE

We know the present participles as words ending in **"-*ing*"**, such as *dancing*, *jumping*, and *singing*. However, unlike its English equivalent, the present participle is not as widely used in French.

These are the different functions of the present participle in French:

- As a verb expressing an action that is related to the main verb of the sentence.

  Example: **<u>Vivant près de la ville,</u> je vais souvent.** (*Living near the city, I go there often.*)

- As a verb used together with the preposition en.

  Example: **Appelle-nous <u>en arrivant</u> chez toi.** (*Call us when you get home.*)

- As an adjective that modifies a noun.

  Example: **le soleil <u>couchant</u>.** (*The setting sun.*)

- As a noun.

  Examples: **un gagnant** (*winner*); **un étudiant** (*student*)

Some rules to remember:

- To form the present participle of **-er**, **-ir**, and **-re** verbs, use the nous form of its present tense and replace the **-ons** ending with **-ant**.

  For example: **donnons** becomes **donnant, mangeons** becomes **mangeant, finissons** becomes **finissant**, and **attendons** becomes **attendant**

- Present participles can never be used to form tenses. Neither can they be used to translate English verb forms literally.

- The present participle cannot be used to talk about something you are currently doing. For that, you must use the present tense.

- When used as an adjective, the present participle has to agree with the noun it describes.

  Example: **des chaises pliantes** (*the folding chairs*)

LET'S PRACTICE!

Exercise 28.1 - Transform the following sentences in this exercise:

Example: Elle travaille et elle chante - <u>Elle travaille en chantant.</u>

   1. Elle écoute Mozart et elle danse   - _____

   2. Elle parle et elle conduit   - _____

   3. Elle sort et elle ferme la porte   - _____

Exercise 28.2 - Choose the correct answer:

   1. Nous discutons en ____ du thé. *(We are talking while drinking tea.)*

     a. boire   b. buvons   c. buvant

   2. Je me suis fait mal en ____ ma langue. *(I hurt myself biting my tongue.)*

     a. mordons   b. mordions   c. mordant

   3. ____ ma glace rapidement, j'ai eu mal aux dents. *(Eating my ice cream fast, I got tooth ache.)*

     a. En mangeant   b. Mangeons   c. Mangions

   4. ____ être sourd, il ne se retourne pas quand je l'appelle. *(Pretending to be deaf, he did not turn around when I call him.)*

     a. Prétendons   b. Prétendant   c. Prétendre

   5. Je fais descendre le Ketchup en ____ la bouteille. *(I get the ketchup down by shaking the bottle.)*

     a. secouant   b. secouons   c. secouer

Exercise 28.3 - Transform these infinitive verbs into present participles:

   1. Vivre   - _____

   2. Couper   - _____

   3. Dormir   - _____

   4. Manger   - _____

   5. Croire   - _____

Exercise 28.4 - Transform these sentences like the example below:

Example: Elle chante et elle danse. - <u>Elle chante en dansant.</u> *(She sings while she's dancing.)*

1. Il fait la cuisine et il danse. *(He cooks and dances.)*

   _____

2. Elle parle et elle rit. *(She talks and laughs.)*

   _____

3. Je parle et je dors. *(I talk and sleep.)*

   _____

4. Il parle au téléphone et conduit sa moto. *(He speaks on the phone and rides his motorcycle.)*

   _____

5. Elle rentre et s'excuse du retard. *(She enters and apologizes for the delay.)*

   _____

Exercise 28.5 - Complete the sentences with the present participles of the verbs in brackets:

1. Ce concours compte beaucoup de candidats _____ (avoir) apporté leur propre gourde. *(This contest has many candidates who have brought their own water bottles.)*

2. Nous cherchons des concepts (différer) _____ de ce qui existe déjà. *(We are looking for concepts differing from what already exists.)*

3. J'étudie souvent le jour (précéder) _____ l'examen. *(I often study the day prededing the exam.)*

4. Il a perdu tout son argent le (miser) _____ sur le mauvais cheval. *(He lost all his money betting on the wrong horse.)*

5. Elle a eu tort en (confier) _____ son secret à Bernard. *(She was wrong confiding her secret to Bernard.)*

Exercise 28.6 - Transform these sentences like the example below:

Example: Je vis à l'étranger. Ma famille me manque beaucoup. - <u>Vivant à l'étranger, ma famille me manque beaucoup.</u> *(Living abroad, I miss my family very much.)*

1. Il a beaucoup de choses à faire. Il n'a pas le temps. *(He has a lot of things to do. He doesn't have time.)*

   _____

2. Je sors du magasin, je paye mes achats. *(I get out of the store. I pay for my purchases.)*

   _____

3. Je prends mon courage à deux mains. Je lui demande de sortir avec moi. *(I gather my courage. I ask her to go out with me.)*

   _____

4. Elle souffre de diabète. Elle doit faire attention à ce qu'elle mange. *(She suffers from diabetes. She has to pay attention to what she eats.)*

   _____

5. J'assiste à des formations en marketing. J'apprends beaucoup de conseils utiles.

   (I attend training in marketing. I'm learning a lot of useful tips.)

   _____

ANSWERS:

Exercise 28.1
Track 77

1/ Elle écoute Mozart en dansant. 2/ Elle parle en conduisant. 3/ Elle sort en fermant la porte.

Exercise 28.2

1/ buvant 2/ mordant 3/ En mangeant 4/ Prétendant 5/ secouant

Exercise 28.3

1/ Vivant 2/ Coupant 3/ Dormant 4/ Mangeant 5/ Croyant

Exercise 28.4

1/ Il fait la cuisine en dansant. 2/ Elle parle en riant. 3/ Je parle en dormant. 4/ Il parle au téléphone en conduisant sa moto. 5/ Elle rentre en s'excusant du retard.

Exercise 28.5

1/ Ce concours compte beaucoup de candidats ayant apporté leur propre gourde . 2/ Nous cherchons des concepts différant de ce qui existe déjà. 3/ J'étudie souvent le jour précédant l'examen. 4/ Il a perdu tout son argent le misant sur le mauvais cheval. 5/ Elle a eu tort en confiant son secret à Bernard.

Exercise 28.6

1/ Ayant beaucoup de choses à faire, il n'a pas le temps. 2/ Sortant du magasin, je paye mes achats. 3/ Prenant mon courage à deux mains, je lui demande de sortir avec moi. 4/ Souffrant de diabète, elle doit faire attention à ce qu'elle mange. 5/ Assistant à des formations en marketing, j'apprends beaucoup de conseils utiles.

DAY 29
"C'EST" AND "IL EST"

Two of the most important impersonal expressions you will come across in French are **"c'est"** and **"il est"**. You have probably heard them already as these are commonly used in giving general comments, such as these:

Track 78

- **C'est magnifique !** (*It's magnificent!*)
- **C'est la vie.** (*That's life.*)
- **Il est intelligent.** (*He is smart.*)
- **C'est facile.** (*It is easy.*)

In English, **c'est** and **il est** could mean *this is, that is, it is,* or *he/she is* and *they are.*

WHEN AND HOW TO USE "C'EST"

- C'est can be used with nouns in this order: **c'est + article + noun or c'est + article + adjective + noun.**

  Some examples:

  - **C'est une bonne idée !** (*That's a good idea!*)
  - **C'est la vie !** (*That's life!*)

- C'est can be used with adjectives: **c'est + adjective.**

  Some examples:

  - **C'est merveilleux !** (*That's wonderful!*)
  - **C'est affreux.** (*That's dreadful.*)

- C'est can be used with names too: **c'est + name.**

  For example:

  - **C'est Jacques.** (*It's Jacques.*)

- C'est can appear with stressed pronouns: **c'est + stressed pronoun or c'est + stressed pronoun + relative clause.**

  Examples:

  - **C'est nous.** (*It is us.*)

- o **C'est moi qui donne le signal.** *(I'm the one who gives the signal.)*

Take note that the verb would have to agree with the pronoun.

- C'est is also used with adverbs: **c'est + modified adverbs.**

  Examples:

  - o **C'est par ici.** *(It's right here.)*
  - o **C'est par là.** *(It's over there.)*

Reminders:

- C'est is supposed to become **ce sont** when used with a plural noun. But in most cases, it is still used as **c'es**t in spoken and informal French.

- C'est is more informal than **il est**.

WHEN AND HOW TO USE "IL EST"

- Il est can be used with a noun pertaining to specific things such as religion, race, or profession. **Il est + noun** (no articles or adjectives come with it).

  Examples:

  - o **Il est français.** *(He is French.)*
  - o **Il est professeur.** *(He is a professor.)*

- Il est can be used with an adjective referring to a person: **Il est + adjective**.

  Examples:

  - o **Il est gentil.** *(He is nice)*
  - o **Elle est jolie.** *(She is pretty.)*

- Il est can also be used with time and expressions related to time: **Il est + time or il est + time expressions.**

  Examples:

  - o **Il est cinq heures.** *(It is 5 o'clock)*
  - o **Il est top tôt.** *(It is too early)*

- Il est is used with prepositional phrases: **il est + prepositional phrase.**

  Examples:

  - o **Il est à l'aéroport.** *(He is at the airport.)*
  - o **Il est ici.** *(He is here.)*

- Il est also appears in some impersonal expressions. This is similar to c'est but more formal.

  Example:

  - **Il est bon d'être avec des amis.** *(It is good to be with friends.)*

Remember:

Il est changes its form depending on the noun it is replacing. It could become **elle est**, **ils sont**, or **elles sont**, depending on how it is used.

"C'EST" VERSUS "IL EST"

Here are some key differences on their respective usage:

- Use c'est with an adjective that describes a situation, and use il est with an adjective that describes a person.

- Use c'est with a noun that has an article or adjective (modified noun), and use il est with a noun that is unmodified.

- Use c'est with a modified adverb, and il est with an unmodified one.

- Use c'est for specific names of people.

- Use il est to cite the location of a person.

- Use il est with time.

- Use c'est in less formal speech.

LET'S PRACTICE!

Exercise 29.1 - Choose the right answer:

1. _____ impossible de trouver un bon emploi. (___ *cannot find a good job.*)

    a. C'est   b. Il est   c. C'est / Il est

2. Mais non, _____ impossible ! *(But no, ___ impossible!)*

    a. c'est   b. il est   c. elle est

3. _____ moi qui ai trouvé la solution. (___ *me who found the solution.)*

    a. C'est   b. Il est   c. Elle est

4. Non, mon frère n'est pas médecin ; _____ professeur. *(No, my brother is not a doctor; ___ teacher.)*

    a. c'est   b. il est   c. A or B

5. Cet homme-là, _____ soldat. *(That man, ___ soldier.)*

    a. c'est   b. il est   c. A or B

> ***Fun fact:*** Stilts were invented in France by shepherds who needed a way to get around in wet marshes.

Exercise 29.2 - Choose the correct answer:

1. ___ cinq heures du soir. *(It's five p.m.)*

    a. C'est   b. Il est

2. ___ ma sœur qui a changé les draps. *(It's my sister that changed the sheets.)*

    a. C'est   b. Il est

3. ___ moins cher que dans l'autre magasin. *(It's cheaper than in the other store.)*

    a. C'est   b. Il est

4. ___ mignon ton nouveau chaton. *(He is cute, your new kitten.)*

    a. C'est   b. Il est

5. ___ impératif que tu comprennes ce que je dis. *(It is imperative that you understand what I'm saying.)*

a. C'est   b. Il est

Exercise 29.3 - Complete the sentences with the correct form of "C'est":

1. _____ magnifique ! *(That's wonderful!)*

2. _____ les deux derniers tickets. *(These are the two last tickets.)*

3. Prends quelques fraises. _____ celles que j'ai cueillies tout à l'heure. *(Take some strawberries. These are the ones I picked earlier.)*

4. Fais-le, _____ une opportunité qui n'arrive qu'une seule fois dans la vie. *(Do it. It's an opportunity that comes only once in a lifetime.)*

5. Viens dire bonjour, _____ Marc et Lucie. *(Come say hi. It's Marc and Lucie.)*

Exercise 29.4 - Complete the sentences with [c'est] or [il est]: (Note: you can write both if both are correct):

1. _____ important de faire attention en traversant la rue. *(It's important to be careful while crossing the street.)*

2. _____ très généreux de ta part. *(It is very generous of you.)*

3. Je crois que _____ trop tard pour regretter cette décision maintenant. *(I think it's too late to regret this decision now.)*

4. Elle dit que _____ de sa faute. *(She says it's his fault.)*

5. Ouvre la porte, _____ mon frère. *(Open the door. It's my brother.)*

ANSWERS:

Exercise 29.1
Track 79

1/ C'est / Il est impossible de trouver un bon emploi. 2/ Mais non, c'est impossible! 3/ C'est moi qui ai trouvé la solution. 4/ Non, mon frère n'est pas médecin ; il est professeur. 5/ Cet homme-là, il est soldat.

Exercise 29.2

1/ Il est 2/ C'est 3/ C'est 4/ Il est 5/ C'est

Exercise 29.3

1/ C'est magnifique ! 2/ Ce sont les deux derniers tickets. 3/ Prends quelques fraises. Ce sont celles que j'ai cueillies tout à l'heure. 4/ Fais-le, c'est une opportunité qui n'arrive qu'une seule fois dans la vie. 5/ Viens dire bonjour, c'est/ce sont Marc et Lucie.

Exercise 29.4

1/ C'est/Il est important de faire attention en traversant le rue. 2/ C'est très généreux de ta part. 3/ Je crois qu'il est/que c'est trop tard pour regretter cette décision maintenant. 4/ Elle dit que c'est de sa faute. 5/ Ouvre la porte, c'est mon frère.

DAY 30
SINGULAR AND PLURAL NOUNS

Here are some of the most important things you need to remember about French nouns.

- French nouns have a gender. To properly use a noun, you have to know if it is masculine or feminine as it will affect your usage of adjectives to modify it, pronouns to replace it, and articles that come before it.

- Adjectives, pronouns, and articles are also affected by whether a noun is in its singular or plural form. These three have to agree with both the count and gender.

- For singular nouns, we use the articles **"le"** or **"un"** for masculine, and **"la"** or **"une"** for feminine.

- For plural nouns, we use **"les"** and **"des"**.

Forming plurals

- Most French nouns can be converted into their plural form by adding **-s**, just as in English.

  Some examples:

    o **le livre** (the books) becomes **les livres** (the books)
    o **un jardin** (a garden) becomes **des jardins** (gardens)

- For singular nouns that already end in **-s**, you no longer need to add an additional **s**.

  For example: **un fils** (a son) is **des fils** (sons) in plural form.

- For singular nouns that end in **-x**, there is no change in the form.

  For example: the plural form of **le prix** (the prize/price) is **les prix** (the prizes/prices).

- Some plural French nouns end in **-x**. These include:

  - plural forms of nouns that end in **-eau** such as **un chapeau** (a hat) which becomes **des chapeaux** (hats).

  - plural forms of nouns that end in **-eu** such as **un jeu** (a game) which becomes **des jeux** (games).

- plural forms of some nouns that in in **-ou** such as **bijou** *(a jewel)* which becomes **des bijoux** *(jewels).*

- In using the word "à" with articles and nouns, remember the following combinations:

  - **à** + **le** becomes **au** (au professeur)

  - **à** + **les** becomes **aux** (aux professeurs)

  - **de** + **le** becomes **du** (du maison)

  - **de** + **les** becomes **des** (des maisons)

LET'S PRACTICE!

Exercise 30.1 - Choose the right answer:

1. Elle écrit ____ lettre. *(She's writing a letter).*

   de? / une? / des? / un?

2. On entendait des _____ dans la pièce voisine. *(Voices could be heard in the next room.)*

   voixs? / vois? / voix? / voies?

3. ____ oiseaux chantent. *(The birds are singing.)*

   Les? / Le? / L'? / La?

4. Ça sert à protéger ses _____. *(It serves to protect your knees.)*

   genou? / genous? / genouz? / genoux?

5. Elle porte ____ lunettes de soleil. *(She's wearing sunglasses.)*

   une? / de? / un? / des?

Exercise 30.2 - Choose the correct answer:

1. Il fait ___ ménage. *(He does the household chores.)*

   a. un   b. une   c. le

2. Nous irons acheter ___ pizzas demain. *(We will go buy pizzas tomorrow.)*

   a. les   b. des   c. de

3. Je n'aime pas ___ soupe. *(I don't like soup.)*

   a. la   b. le   c. un

4. Elle a pris ___ bateau pour aller en Angleterre. *(She took a boat to go to England.)*

   a. le   b. un   c. une

5. As-tu ___ couteaux ? *(Do you have the knives?)*

   a. des   b. unes   c. les

Exercise 30.3 - Complete the table below with the correct form for each noun:

Singular	Plural
	Des livres *(books)*
Une maison *(a house)*	
Un chapeau *(a hat)*	
	Des chevaux *(horses)*
Un jeu *(a game)*	

Exercise 30.4 - Complete the sentences with [le[, [la] or [les]:

1. J'ai oublié _____ clés de mon bureau à la maison. *(I forgot the keys to my office at home.)*

2. Il va garer _____ voiture près de la porte. *(He's going to park the car near the door.)*

3. Tu vas tout droit, puis tu tournes à gauche après _____ rond-point. *(You go straight and then turn left after the roundabout.)*

4. J'ai cherché _____ lunettes de soleil partout. *(I looked for the sunglasses everywhere.)*

5. J'ai déjà abandonné mes résolutions de _____ nouvelle année. *(I already abandoned my new year's resolutions.)*

Exercise 30.5 - Complete the sentences with [un], [une] or [des]:

1. J'ai offert _____ fleurs à ma mère. *(I offered flowers to my mother.)*

2. Il a _____ gros appétit. *(He has a big appetite.)*

3. Elle a _____ crampes à l'estomac. *(She has stomach cramps.)*

4. Nous voulons faire _____ tour du monde. *(We want to do a world tour.)*

5. Rappelle-moi d'acheter _____ nouvelle ampoule. *(Remind me to buy a new light bulb.)*

Exercise 30.6 - Complete the sentences with [le], [la], [les], [un], [une] or [des]:

1. J'écris _____ lettre à mon correspondant. *(I'm writing a letter to my pen pal.)*

2. Chaque fois qu'il passe devant _____ pâtisserie, il doit acheter _____ croissant. *(Everytime he passes in front of the pastry he has to buy a croissant.)*

3. J'ai acheté _____ Lego pour l'anniversaire de mon neveu. *(I bought Legos for my nephew's birthday.)*

4. _____ coucher du soleil est le meilleur moment de _____ journée. *(The sunset is the best moment of the day.)*

5. Nous sommes partis faire _____ promenade au bord de _____ mer. *(We went on a walk by the sea shore.)*

ANSWERS:

Exercise 30.1
Track 80

1/ Elle écrit une lettre. 2/ On entendait des voix dans la pièce voisine. 3/ Les oiseaux chantent. 5/ Ça sert à protéger ses genoux. 6/ Elle porte des lunettes de soleil.

Exercise 30.2:

1/ le 2/ des 3/ la 4/ un 5/ les

Exercise 30.3

Singular	Plural
Un livre	Des livres
Une maison	Des maisons
Un chapeau	Des chapeaux
Un cheval	Des chevaux
Un jeu	Des jeux

Exercise 30.4

1/ J'ai oublié les clés de mon bureau à la maison. 2/ Il va garer la voiture près de la porte. 3/ Tu vas tout droit, puis tu tournes à gauche après le rond-point. 4/ J'ai cherché les lunettes de soleil partout. 5/ J'ai déjà abandonné mes résolutions de la nouvelle année.

Exercise 30.5

1/ J'ai offert des fleurs à ma mère. 2/ Il a un gros appétit. 3/ Elle a des crampes à l'estomac. 4/ Nous voulons faire un tour du monde. 5/ Rappelle-moi d'acheter une nouvelle ampoule.

Exercise 30.6

1/ J'écris une lettre à mon correspondant. 2/ Chaque fois qu'il passe devant la pâtisserie, il doit acheter un croissant. 3/ J'ai acheté des Lego pour l'anniversaire de mon neveu. 4/ Le coucher du soleil est le meilleur moment de la journée. 5/ Nous sommes partis faire une promenade au bord de la mer.

BONUS!

BONUS TOPICS

I. Using "c'est..que" / "qui" sentence structure for emphasis

Highlighting something in your speech is quite easy when speaking in English: all you need to do is say the word slower or louder than the rest of the sentence. In French, this is called **"accent tonique"** or *"tonic accent"*, and one of the ways to use this is to change the sentence structure by using "c'est...que" / "qui".

Here's how:

- Instead of the usual subject + verb + object structure, you twist things around using c'est + noun/stressed pronoun + que/qui clause.

  For example:

  Instead of saying **elle aime Tom** *(she likes Tom)*, you say **"C'est Tom qu'elle aime"** which is equivalent to *"it is Tom that she likes"*. This way, Tom is being emphasized.

- In place of the noun to be highlighted, you can also use stressed pronouns (see previous lesson about this).

  For example: **C'est moi qui l'aime.** *(It is ME who likes him.)*

- For an even more dramatic and highly emphatic way of saying things, you can make use of both specific noun and stressed pronoun.

  For example: **Tom, c'est lui qu'elle aime !** *(Tom, it's him that she likes!)*

II. Cardinal numbers versus ordinal numbers

The difference:

- Cardinal numbers are used to tell us how many, or what quantity, there are. They are used in counting.

  Example: 1, 2, 3, 4 and so on.

- Ordinal numbers tell us the position or the order in relation to other numbers. They are used in classifying things.

  Example: 1st, 2nd, 3rd, 4th, and so on.

- For more of this, check out the lesson for day 27 on numbers.

III. Dates and Days

How to say the date:

- Use this format: C'est + le + day of the month + month.

- For the day of the month, you use the cardinal numbers 2 to 31.

- For the first day of the month, you use the ordinal number "1st". Or in French, premier which is abbreviated as "1er".

    Examples:

    - **C'est le 4 septembre 2020.**
    - **C'est le premier novembre.**
    - **C'est le 1er novembre.**

- In informal speech, you can say "On est" or "Nous sommes" instead of "C'est".

    Examples: **On est le 15 octobre. Nous sommes le premier mars.**

The days of the week:
Track 81

Day	In French	Pronunciation
Monday	lundi	luhn-DEE
Tuesday	mardi	mahr-DEE
Wednesday	mercredi	mehr-kruh-DEE
Thursday	jeudi	juh-DEE
Friday	vendredi	vahn-druh-DEE
Saturday	samedi	sahm-DEE
Sunday	dimanche	dee-MAHNSH

Note: unlike in English, the first letters of the days of the week (les jours de la semaine) aren't capitalised in French.

How to ask the date:

Track 82

- **Quelle est la date ?** *(What is the date?)*

- **Quelle est la date aujourd'hui ?** *(What's the date today?)*

- **On est le combien aujourd'hui ?** *(What's today's date?)*

- **Quel jour sommes-nous ?** *(What day is it?)*
- **Quand ?** *(When?)*

IV. Telling the time

How to ask the time

Say: " **Quelle heure est-il ?** " It is pronounced as *kell eurh eh teel?* Meaning, *"what's the time?"* or *"what time is it?"*

The format

Il est (insert number of hours) heure(s) (insert number of minutes). This format applies to both 12—hour clock and 24-hour clock.

Examples:

Track 83

- **Il est une heure.** *(It is one o'clock.)*
- **Il est cinq heures douze.** *(It is twelve minutes past 5.)*

You can abbreviate the time by placing the letter *h* in between the time and minutes.

For example: 9h37 for 9:37 and 10h00 for 10 o'clock.

If you are going to only write down the minutes, use "min" after the number.

For example: 37 min.

V. The Weather

Track 84

- **le temps** – *weather*
- **la météo** – *weather forecast*

To ask about the weather, you can say:

Track 85
Quel temps fait-il ?
Possible answers :

Il fait... (It's...)	chaud *(hot)* froid *(cold)* frais *(cool)* beau *(nice)* mauvais *(bad)* humide *(humid)* nuageux *(cloudy)* orageux *(stormy)*
Il y a... (It's)	du brouillard *(foggy)* du soleil *(sunny)*
Il y a... (it's)	Du vent *(windy)*
Il... (it's)	pleut *(raining)* pleut à verse (pouring) neige *(snowing)* gèle *(freezing)*

VI. The Different Seasons and Months
Track 86

le printemps *(spring)*	l'automne *(autumn)*
l'été *(summer)*	l'hiver *(winter)*

The months of the year:

Month	In French
January	janvier
February	février
March	mars
April	avril
May	mai
June	juin
July	juillet

August	août
September	septembre
October	octobre
November	novembre
December	décembre

VII. Expressing Quantity

Here is a list of vocabulary pertaining to quantities, weights, and measures.

Track 87

une bouteille de	*bottle*	un carton de	*box*
une cuillère à soupe de	*tablespoon*	une cuillère à thé / café de	*teaspoon*
un kilogramme de / un kilo de	*kilogram*	un litre de	*liter*
une livre de	*pound*	un mille	*mile*
un pied	*foot*	un pot de	*jar, cup*
un pouce	*inch*	une tasse de	*cup*
un verre de	*glass*	assez (de)	*quite, fairly, enough*
autant (de)	*as much, as many*	beaucoup (de)	*a lot, many*
bien de	*quite a few*	combien (de)	*how many, much*
davantage	*more*	encore de	*more*
environ	*around, approximately*	la majorité de	*the majority of*
la minorité de	*the minority of*	moins (de)	*less, fewer*

CONCLUSION

You didn't think I would just end this book without saying goodbye properly, did you? Of course not! Proper goodbyes are terribly important now that we have been through a lot of grammar-y stuff these last 30 days. That kind of huge thing warrants a heartfelt farewell.

So here are some points I'd like to add before we go our separate ways.

1. I'd love to hear from you! Would it be too much to ask what you think about this book? If you can spare a few minutes, do let me know your thoughts by sending an email to contact@talkinfrench.com. Not only would I be delighted to receive your response, I would also like to know how I could be of further help, and how I could make an even better book for all French language learners.

2. I hope you will stick to the habit of learning French each day. In this book, I have neatly divided the lessons into small daily tasks for you, hoping that the learning habit will stick. Did it work? I sure hope it did.

3. Learning French can absolutely be hard. After teaching it for so many years, I truly get that, and that's why I have been labouring to make this book as unboring as I can. The key is to focus on the fun parts. Like making it your new hobby, for example. I'll be here to guide you as best as I can.

And so with that, we say our goodbyes.

À bientôt, mon ami !

Frederic

AUDIO DOWNLOAD INSTRUCTIONS

Copy and paste this link into your browser:

https://www.talkinfrench.com/audio-grammar-beginner/

- Click on the book cover. It will take you to a Dropbox folder containing each individual file. (If you're not familiar with what Dropbox is or how it works, don't panic, it just a storage facility.)

- Click the DOWNLOAD button in the Dropbox folder located in the upper right portion of your screen. A box may pop up asking you to sign in to Dropbox. Simply click, "No thanks, continue to download" under the sign-in boxes. (If you have a Dropbox account, you can choose to save it to your own Dropbox so you have access anywhere via the internet.)

- The files you have downloaded will be saved in a .zip file. Note: This is large file. Don't try opening it until your browser tells you that it has completed the download successfully (usually a few minutes on a broadband connection but if your connection is unreliable, it could take 10 to 20 minutes).

- The files will be in your "downloads" folder unless you have changed your settings. Extract them from the folder and save them to your computer or copy to your preferred devices, *et voilà !* You can now listen to the audio anytime, anywhere.

ABOUT THE AUTHOR

Frédéric Bibard is the founder of TalkInFrench.com.

He spent several years teaching French while traveling abroad and has since moved back to Paris to dedicate his time to developing fun and helpful French language resources.

He takes food seriously (he is French after all), but he complements it with a love of running which allows him to nurture his passion for good food while staying in shape.

Say hello to him at contact@talkinfrench.com or www.talkinfrench.com.

Made in the USA
Las Vegas, NV
29 March 2021